European
Contemporary
Houses

European Contemporary Houses

THE ART OF THE HABITAT

Series directed by Olivier Boissière

Front cover
A house in Barcelona,
Spain. Architect:
Joan Rodón.

Back cover
A house in Düsseldorf,
Germany. Architect:
Wolfgang Döring.

Page 2
A house in Majorca,
Spain. Architect:
Pere Nicolau.

Publisher editor: Jean-François Gonthier
Art director: Bruno Leprince
Cover design: Daniel Guerrier
Editing staff: Hortense Lyon, Charles Bilas, Véronique Donnat
Translation: Rubye Monet, Unity Woodman
Assistant to the publisher: Sophie-Charlotte Legendre
Correction and revision: Françoise Derray
Composition: Graffic, Paris
Filmsetting: Compo Rive Gauche, Paris
Lithography: ARCO Editorial, Barcelone

This edition copyright © TELLERI, PARIS 1998
All illustrations copyright © ARCO Editorial except for front and back cover © TELLERI
ISBN : 2-7450-0026-8
Printed in the European Union

TELLERI - 30, rue de Charonne - F 75011 Paris

Contents

Introduction

We are apt to remember this fin de siècle as the apogee of progress and its subsequent dramatic changes in lifestyle, despite the violent upheavals, revolutions and acceleration of history that have marked this century.

The house with its technological evolution in comfort is emblematic of our times and, for many of us, owning a house is still an important aspiration, especially with the growing spread of urbanization. Yet who could have imagined, even a few decades ago, the choices we now have, the sophisticated air-conditioning, the marvels of home appliances or the practicality of self-cleaning ovens?

Modern architecture has naturally integrated these advances in technology and taken full advantage of today's innovative construction techniques. Architects work with more versatile and effective materials than ever before, making for flexible layouts and houses that open out to embrace the landscape. No longer armed with a set of doctrinaire principles to convince us of its worth – the symptom of Modernism's infancy – European architecture tends to express the spirit of a place, without insisting upon what is "up-to-date."

With Europe's diverse landscapes, topographies, climates and cultures, it is not surprising that its late 20th-century architects have chosen to express their talent by highlighting the context of a site, using local materials with discernment and taking bold steps in response to a given situation. And they do so without compromising on innovation, or giving in to pastiches or the morose delights of copying, making for houses that express the idioms of a diverse and well-tempered modernity, of which some of the best illustrations are presented in this book.

Modern European architecture is characterized by a strict rational approach, imbued with a sense of place, whereby the structure naturally takes up the landscape. A house in Loco, Switzerland, by architect Luigi Snozzi.

A house in Stuttgart, Germany

Is there an architect in the house? Except for its size and its location in a residential suburb of Stuttgart, one might think that this was the cabin of a Schrebergärten, one of those workers' gardens that are found all over Germany, where the owner slaps together a shelter with whatever materials come to hand.

Charlotte House is nonetheless the work of an architect, and not of the lesser ones either: Günter Behnisch has to his credit the German Parliament building in Bonn, the Olympic Park in Munich with its famous roof (realized together with Frei Otto) as well as an impressive number of schools, corporation offices and residential buildings. Born in 1922, he opened his first agency in Stuttgart in 1952 and built the greater part of his career in Germany where he distinguished himself as one of the pioneers in using methods of prefabrication. His recent works show an evolution toward an architecture conceived as a grouping of independent planes fragmented and joined together with the greatest flexibility of association.

The half-moon shape of the west front looks out onto the street.

Opposite page
A most unusual roof peeps out of the surrounding vegetation.

Several steps lead up to the entrance on the north side of the house.

On the threshold, the stone is encrusted with bits of sparkling color.

Opposite page
Scale model showing the sunken swimming pool behind large windows.

The houses stand close to each other, on small plots of land.

The roof is equipped with solar panels for storing energy.

Though set quite apart, Charlotte House shares with Behnisch's public work that freedom of spirit that places it in the line of spontaneous architecture and gives it the casual appearance of a work that has been successful through pure chance. It is a house that wants to look as if it had no architect, as if it had rebelled against all aesthetic principles. Except that one perceives the distant echo of the youth center built by Jean Prouvé in the Paris suburb of Ermont or the house Pierre Chareau did on Long Island for the painter Motherwell.

From a distance, the house resembles nothing more than a giant oil drum lying on its side in the middle of a tangle of shrubbery. Not a very romantic image, but a love match all the same. For the sunflowers growing at the edge of the terrace and the sheet metal of the roof both seek the sun: the former by turning their heads to catch the rays, the latter in the form of solar panels attached to its round surface. Partially buried on its north side as a protection from the cold, the building is wide open toward the south on an indoor swimming pool sunk below ground level. Behnisch does not hide his espousal of the protest ideas of the late 1960s, which gave priority to ecology and made use of recycled materials and natural resources, a way of thinking that has become a reflex in Germany.

Everything about the house seems to denote a certain disorder. Does one sense a slight provocation to the surrounding houses? All four sides are different – the entrance facade on the north has a certain symmetry, with its door, two windows with sliding shutters and a little dormer window. The one facing the street presents a heterogeneous collection of windows, shutters and balustrades of all sizes and shapes. The remaining two sides, while surely the fruit of highly complicated rules of composition, escape all attempts at any orthodox classification.

Inside reigns an ecological spirit that has little to do with design or aesthetic orders. Behnisch combines wood and wicker, Indian fabrics and Provencal prints with traditional furniture in a warm and sensual atmosphere. The dark corners, sliding doors, balconies, ladders and mezzanines compose a universe out of a childhood dream. But perhaps the child in question dreamed of being an aviator, for beneath its apparent complexity, Charlotte House has all the simplicity of an airplane hangar, which makes it also a worthy heir to modern architecture. □

View from the living room, extended by a terrace.

The dining room forms a single space with the kitchen.

Upper floor
1. Bedroom
2. Bedroom
3. Bedroom
4. Bathroom
5. Shower-room
6. Bathroom

Ground floor
1. Entrance
2. Kitchen
3. Living room
4. Verandah
5. Bedroom
6. Toilet
7. Pantry
8. Parking

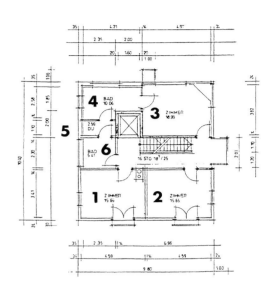

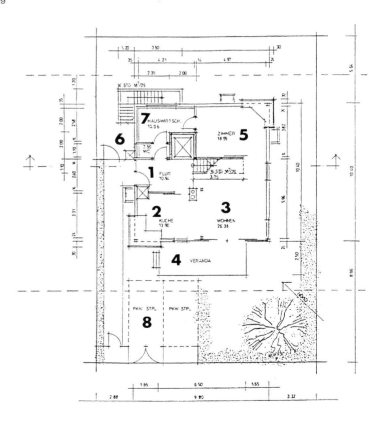

An old-fashioned stove adds a rustic note to the decor.

In the dining room.
Illuminated by the sun,
the wood takes on a
blond glow.

Detail of the staircase
showing the
balustrade.

View of one of the
bedrooms showing a
part of the
extraordinary barrel
vault.

14 A house in Stuttgart, Germany

An atmosphere that
belongs very much to the
1970s, with bright colors
and natural wood.

Daniel Spreng

A house in Bern, Switzerland

On the west front, a modest door set back between broad windows faces the garden. The chimney on the roof proudly wears the form and color of industrial aesthetics.

Opposite page
The building with its rooftop addition topped by a glass pyramid has two sources of light, laterally and from above. Each floor is individualized through use of different materials.

Amid the villas of Länggasse, a residential quarter of Bern, the little building by Daniel Spreng looks rather like a mutant. Compact, drawn in on itself, it wears with elegance the modesty of its origins: a former workshop that has been converted into a house quite unlike those around it, offering a viable alternative to the classic type of private home.

The first visible sign of the architect's endeavor is the stainless steel cube placed on the roof-terrace of the original structure, a clear affirmation that he has opted for the aesthetics of industrial architecture. On the ground floor the irregular pentagon of concrete has been given a second skin of gray brick, trimmed with a broad strip of pale pink running along its upper part. This two-tone effect lends the place a slightly offbeat look, a restrained Swiss touch of fantasy in a project that is otherwise both rigorous and respectful of the environment.

The upper story is topped by a skylight in the shape of a glass pyramid that echoes the four-sided sloping roofs of the neighboring houses. Through this glass roof the light streams in, flooding the entire level (which includes a spacious bedroom further extended by a terrace) and bathing the staircase to form a large well of light in the center of the living room. The space is completely open, structured by a line that

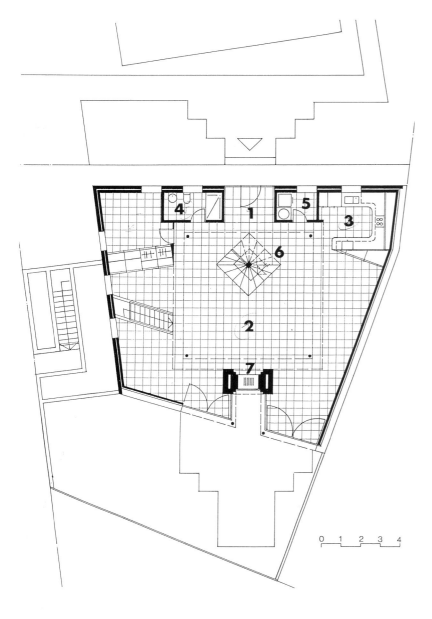

runs from the entrance to the fireplace unit and ends in the tiny garden on the west. It is also the axis of symmetry of the square formed by the upper floor and marked at the four corners by slim supporting columns.

Except for the bedroom with adjoining bath and the kitchen, situated on either side of the entrance, the entire ground floor is laid out around this imprint of the upper story. A square formed by bands of light is also visible on the floor, entering through the narrow glass strip that runs around the base of the cube, up above on the terrace. This defines the center of the house, a clever way to recall, within the open space characteristic of industrial architecture, the memory of the enclosed space of a traditional home. It is also a way of playing with light and with a particular form, the square, that reappears in endless guises: in the treatment of the floor, the shape of the windows, the modern version of a coffered ceiling or the volume of the fireplace.

Everywhere the architect affirms his love of sharp lines and acute angles, even in the oblique corners of the spiral staircase. His utterly rigorous manner makes no concession to the curve, a style perfectly suited by the discreet color scheme and well-defined by the white and gray tones of the lacquered bricks and the dark slate of the floors. □

Ground floor
1. Entrance
2. Living room
3. Kitchen
4. Bathroom
5. Pantry
6. Staircase
7. Fireplace

The plan shows how the volumes have been superimposed: the initial polygon, the cube and the glass pyramid.

Opposite page
Different in appearance, yet without ostentation, the house remains in the spirit of the surrounding constructions.

The bedroom, simple and
understated, enjoys a dual
extension - outward to the
terrace and upward to the sky.

Opposite page
On the ground floor, space is the
priority – a single space,
unbroken by any walls. The
decoration is essentially a matter
of enlivening the surfaces. The
black furniture underscores even
further the studied sobriety of
the entire construction.

The metal staircase displays its sculptured forms in the central
axis of the house, which runs from the front door to the door of
the garden.

Opposite page
The entrance seen from the dining room, a harmony in black
and white, varying with the light that comes down from above.

The bedroom is a luminous open space, where the white tiled
bathroom seems to be part of the furniture.

Elio Di Franco

A house in Florence, Italy

A verdant haven of peace, just a stone's throw from the center of Florence.

Opposite page
Sober and sophisticated in the Italian manner, under azure skies. The house is open on the garden, like an invitation to spend one's life out of doors.

Could it be that the ghost of Filippo Brunelleschi comes to haunt all Florentine architects? Modern houses are few and far between in the city of the Medicis and this villa recently recomposed by Elio Di Franco, based on an existing structure dating from the 1960s, is one of the rare exceptions that prove the rule. It stands at the southern edge of Florence, just beyond the Porta San Giorgio that leads to the foot of the Forte di Belvedere near the Boboli Gardens. Between town and country, the site commands a panoramic view northward over the red tile roofs dominated by the Cathedral and plunging to the south toward San Miniato al Monte. The cypress trees that rise beside it herald the start of the rolling Tuscan hills.

A modern villa then, but which nonetheless bears distant memories of the Renaissance, like its smooth finish and its cornice in the manner of a Florentine palazzo. As for the triple arched portico on two slim columns, it would not dream of hiding its affiliations with the vocabulary of ancient architecture. The little round windows resemble ancient medallions and at the same time recall the little round porthole-like windows used by the previous architect.

Faced with this dual heritage, Elio Di Franco puts forward

an idea that is both simple and strong, inspired by the site and the natural landscape so nearby. He has chosen to open up the walls and to play on interpenetration of inside and outside.

From the entrance porchway on the north, the axial perspective leads to the light-flooded garden at the rear. A tiered structure on the left marks the location of the staircase going up to the pergola. On the ground floor the blond *pietra serena* is uninterrupted from floor to terrace.

But there is also communication in the harmony of the formal language, in the the play of correspondences of pure geometric forms, the circle, the rectangle and the square. On the south, the openings are inscribed within two equal squares that make up for the otherwise asymmetrical layout of the facade. The round arches surmounted by three square windows and united by a horizontal band are repeated identically on the entrance facade.

Sober by day, the villa becomes a spectacle at night through its lighting: an extroverted house created for a fashion designer. Here a mirror in which the house is reflected. There, a staircase, framed by the central arch, with serpentine lines that evoke the ripple of silk. And upstairs, where the bedrooms and bath are lodged in irregular volumes, the dominant material is Carrara marble. □

Framed by the arcades, a male torso and a staircase with feminine curves, a subtle staging that leaves nothing to chance.

The geometric purity of the wall masking the staircase that leads up to the pergola.

Opposite page
The gracefully tapered columns of the entrance add a discreet sensuality to the polished flagstones of *pietra serena*.

Sheltered from the sun, this intimate lounge is like a space
half indoors and half out. The sofa echoes the color of the
stone, the rug copies the shape of the pool.

Opposite page
The flagstone terrace, like an extension of the ground floor.

At night, the balanced asymmetry of the facade is clearly
seen, along with its reflection in the circular pool.

Refinement and
attention to detail are
visible in this staircase
leading to the
bedrooms.

The luxury of everyday
life: a view of the
Tuscan countryside
from the bathtub.

Wolfgang Döring

A house in Düsseldorf, Germany

The facade on the
garden, punctuated by
metal pillars.

Opposite page
With its simple
volumes and visible
structural supports, this
house clearly proclaims
its industrial aesthetics.

All the beauty of a brand-new factory building. But beneath its forbidding exterior lies the heart of a village house built in the style of the country... and the style of the country is wholeheartedly industrial! Wittlaer is only a few kilometers from Düsseldorf, near the main centers of German heavy industry. The architect Wolfgang Döring opened his offices here in 1964 after getting his start in one of the largest agencies of the time, the Schneider-Esleben agency. He has to his credit private houses, hotels, commercial complexes, and of course, industrial buildings. In addition to his activities as a teacher, Wolfgang Döring has built extensively both in Germany and abroad.

Certainly the ancestor of this house would be the one that Charles Eames built at Los Angeles' Pacific Palisades, using industrial components. But the intentional mimicry of industry is much clearer here, perhaps because the inhabitants, taking their example from New York lofts, have better learned the lesson of the freedom offered by the vast spaces without visual barriers.

The plan of the house has the childlike simplicity of a Meccano or erector set construction. A large rectangle surmounted by a smaller rectangle, which is flanked by a

Plan

1. Entrance
2. Living room
3. Dining room
4. Study
5. Bedroom
6. Bedroom
7. Kitchen
8. Bathroom
9. Toilet
10. Terrace
11. Garage

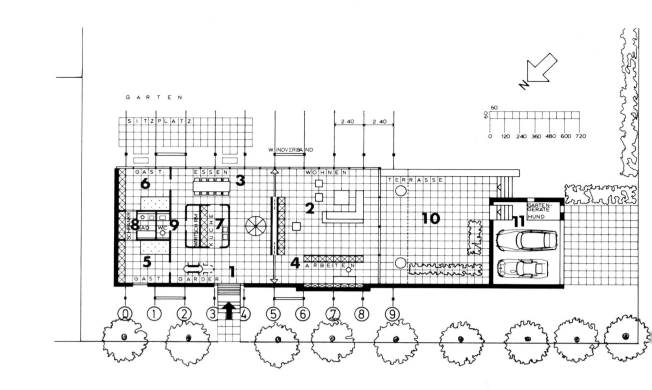

cylinder placed off-center along one side. The metal structure of the building, painted a triumphant red, is visible on the outside of the walls. Paradoxically, the vertical punctuation it gives to the facade only adds to the horizontality of the composition. The house seems anchored to the ground in the defensive attitude of a fortress. Even the canopy over the entrance has an uncanny resemblance to a drawbridge.

You enter on the north side, from the street, where a solid wall of concrete bricks with a band of aluminum in its upper part runs around the entire building. On the garden side, the facade has a line of sliding windows that give access to the terrace on the west.

The inner space consists of a single unbroken volume, without pillars or sustaining walls. Precisely-placed partitions define the different zones of occupation of the space. At the eastern end, two guest bedrooms separated by a bathroom; in the axis of the entrance hall, the dining room; to the west, giving onto the terrace and garage, a large space shared by the living room and study, separated by a bookcase wall. The bedroom upstairs is accessible from a spiral staircase, marked on outside by its cylindrical casing. Seen from the inside, the black lines of its metal structure contrast strangely with the round-edged white cube that holds the kitchen. This is the only space in the house that announces itself as a closed area, yet it is far from impenetrable, as three of its sides open with sliding doors. With its hi-tech cylindrical cupboard, this kitchen cube is a perfect echo to the volumes placed on the roof.

From floor to ceiling, surfaces covered with brick or tile, metal beams, sections of corrugated iron and assorted lighting tracks create a diversity of lines, grids and patterns that scramble the perspectives and fill the visual space. Compared to these patterns from a virtual universe, the classic modern pieces – Le Corbusier sofa and armchairs, Breuer chairs – seem very sedate indeed. □

A metallic spiral staircase contrasts with the straight lines that dominate elsewhere.

Opposite page
Plan of the house: a vast open space without walls.

This cube with rounded edges contains the kitchen.

Living room and study area,
separated by bookshelves,
share the same space under an
imposing metallic structure.

Opposite page
The classic modern
Le Corbusier sofa
and armchairs, for conversing
or contemplating the
surrounding landscape through
the entirely glazed facade.

A house at Lyon-Vaise, France

This house was built entirely of prefabricated units. The roof was assembled in a single day.

Opposite page
The huge awning serves as a protection against rain.

Anyone who has ever, intentionally or unwittingly, trampled a flower bed knows the ravages that weight inflicts on living plants. Anyone who sets out to build 200 square meters of living space in a country garden without harming a blade of grass would do well to say a prayer, or else they had better have a good imagination, not to mention an excellent knowledge of the laws of physics. Françoise-Hélène Jourda and Gilles Perraudin have both.

Engineers as well as architects, they have placed their faith in technical progress, at least the sort that opens the way to new harmony with nature. Although they are confirmed ecologists who believe that architecture should respect the environment, Jourda and Perraudin do not advocate a return to the land and to vernacular architecture. To create structures that rival the finesse of nature itself, they make use of complex calculations and the virtues of composite materials. Graduates of the Lyon School of Architecture, designers of the new architecture school of Vaulx-en-Velin, they are strongly implanted in the Lyon region, as well as in Germany where so-called "bioclimatic" architecture has found favor for many years.

The house located in Vaise was designed for the architect couple and their four children. It has the general shape of a

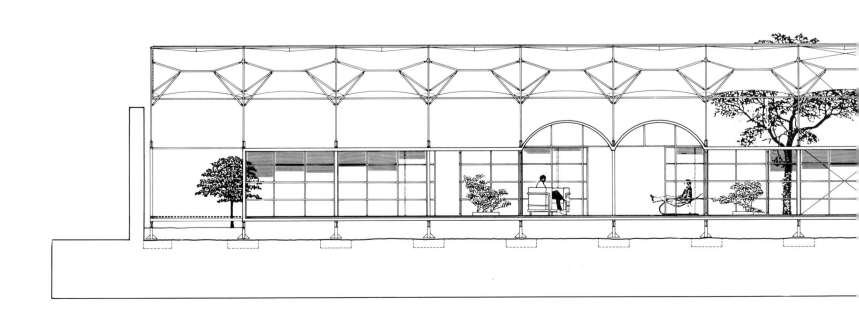

40 A house at Lyon-Vaise, France

The walls give way to
let in light and air.

Cross-section :
entrance, bathroom,
living room, outdoor
terrace.

Opposite page
A series of glazed
modules give rhythm to
the facade facing the
garden.

Longitudinal cross-
section of the living
areas.

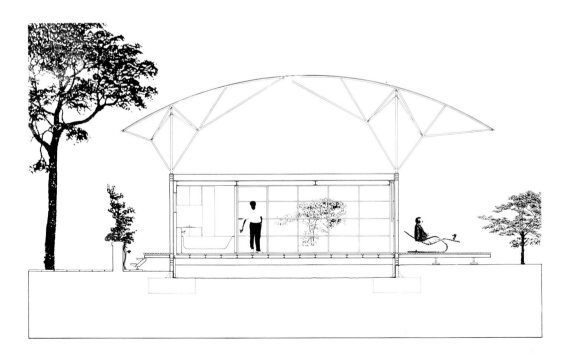

large market stall placed sideways on its plot of land, enclosed by walls and bordered on the west by the street. Built on a raised platform supported on piles, the house does not rest on the ground at all and gives the impression of floating. Thus, the vegetation is preserved and the house is ventilated, able to breathe from the foundations to the roof. The latter, detached from the habitat itself, stretches its protective wing like an immense umbrella over the terraces that border the house. The metal ribs reach upward like the limbs of a tree, a movement echoed by a row of plane trees in the background.

The reference to a living organism, however, lies less in the shape than in the spirit of the undertaking. The house of Jourda and Perraudin is a structure that evolves and transforms. Additional spaces can be integrated as needed between the roof and the ceiling. Inside the prefabricated metal cage that forms the main structure, the volumes can be modified at will. The house has not been built for eternity – the materials that compose it are for the most part biodegradable.

The interior shell is no more than a box, closed on three sides and open the entire length of the fourth, with a southern exposure. This side, with its warm wooden panels and rounded vaults, contrasts sharply with the stark metallic lines of the rest of the house. The bedrooms, living room and kitchen share the seven modules giving on the garden – all identical and all equipped with removable sliding glass panels, which offer a thousand and one ways to dialogue with light, sun, rain and wind. An extension of the terrace reaches outward toward the tall pine trees, like a hand outstretched to the exterior, carrying the message of an architecture reconciled with its environment. □

The living room area
extends onto the terrace:
the garden is visible all in
every direction.

Opposite page
Glass partitions, here around
the library, can be modified
at will.

The lines of a Le Corbusier's
reclining chair recall the
structure of the roof.

The dining area in the foreground and the living room form a single space. In the rear, the transparent, movable partitions open on the office.

A half wall delimits the space devoted to the kitchen.
Opposite page
View of the living room from the terrace. The vaulted wooden ceiling adds warmth and comfort. The television area can be isolated by a sliding screen.

A house in Rotterdam, The Netherlands

The front of the house faces north. The eastern side is protected from the sun by a sliding screen.

Opposite page
The house, seen here from the south, is built on a canal. The reeds along the water find their rightful place in this architecture all of lightness and transparency.

The arm of a canal, a piece of yellow wall, a broad swathe of sky... who can avoid thinking of Vermeer? Especially since the architectural agency Mecanoo was also born in Delft. The name is an allusion to the famous building toy, Meccano; it was also the title of a magazine of the early 1920s, directed by Van Doesburg, which heralded the De Stijl movement and diffused the spirit of Dada in the Netherlands.

This house, built in Rotterdam by Erik Van Egeraat and Francine Houben, harks back to these distant ancestors. The rupture with the brick houses with their pointed gables against which it stands was begun long ago. The narrow space between them is not a gap, it is a chasm. Van Egeraat and Houben practice the unabashed modernism that has become a Dutch tradition ever since the innovative experiments of the architects Berlage and Oud at the turn of the century.

From south to north the eye plunges directly through the glass walls into a landscape of sky and water, barely stopping on its trajectory in the living room or the bedroom that one can make out just above. The predominant fluidity, together

with the style of the architecture, works without lyricism but with a sort of magic to effectively abolish the inner space. The north front overlooks the lake of Kralinge Plas. The front door is modest, on a human scale, beside the solid concrete wall that runs the entire height of the building.

The architects have handled the facade like an abstract composition, using the glass and concrete in zones of flat color and wielding the steel as if it were a pencil point. The windows continue on the eastern wall. A bamboo curtain filters the light and opens at will on the glass screen where are played out, large as life, scenes from the daily life of a family of architects. The sets, a mix of concrete and wood, are the bedrooms and the library, beneath which spreads out a vast space that serves as a combination living room/dining room/kitchen. Between the two levels a staircase shows its accordion profile against a wood-covered wall.

Need one even go inside? The interior seems to hold no mystery: the internal bareness repeats the transparency of the outer shell. All around, the various areas are laid out in a spatial and visual continuity that clearly shows the function of each one.

On the ground floor, unlike the rest of the house, the opaqueness of its concrete walls conceals a space propitious to work and concentration. It opens southward onto a pebble-paved Zen garden, with a small pool at one end in the form of a perfect circle. From this microcosm of stone and water emanates an aura of Japan that permeates the rest of the house. It is omnipresent: in the lightness of the structure, the asymmetry of the facades, the walls cut out like sliding panels, the bamboo and tropical wood.

While down at the end of the garden, the canal flows quietly on… □

The monumental
impact of the concrete
panel contrasts with
the transparency of the
glass. A round opening
in the overhanging roof
breaks the opacity and
forms a well of light.

Spectacular view of
Kralinge Plas lake from
the library.

On the ground floor
wood, concrete and
glass form a mosaic
right up to the canal.

Longitudinal cross-
section: the spaces
hinge on a central void
two stories high.
1. Facade/Entrance
2. Lower living
room/study
3. Zen garden
4. Upper living room
5. Kitchen
6. Open air terrace
7. Library
8. Bedroom

Opposite page
Space without visual
barriers enables one to
see the living room and
library at the same
time.

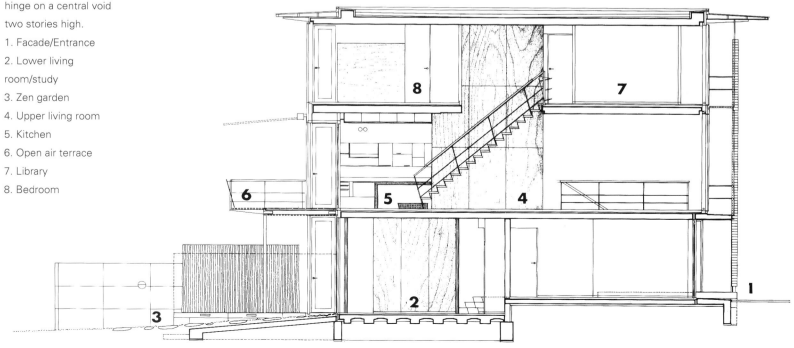

Beth Gali

A house in Barcelona, Spain

In a profession largely dominated by a male establishment hardly eager to give up any of the privileges of its class or sex, women architects owe their recognition to unquestionable competence. Women have come a long way since the days when a Julia Morgan owed her career to the protection of the magnate Randolph Hearst. Alison Smithson in England, Denise Scott Brown in the United States, the Iraqi Zaha Hadid and the Japanese Itsuko Hasegawa have shown (if they really needed to prove it) that women in the world of architecture were a new force to be reckoned with.

Beth Gali belongs to this generation. From project to realization, she has been able to impose her manner and her talent. Honors and awards show the respect she has earned in the eyes of her fellow architects. Today she occupies the post of chief architect for the city of Barcelona, heads the school of urban design of the university of architecture and in addition to all this, find the time to build.

Once limited to the coastal strip, Barcelona has in recent years gradually invaded the slopes of the nearby mountains.

Prismatic windows protrude from the facade, offering the bedrooms a 180° view on Mount Tibidabo.

Opposite page
Alternately massive or transparent, this house makes use of contrasting shapes and materials, the better to provide for the comfort of its inhabitants.

You have only to push
the sliding door to get
from the office to the
marble-edged
swimming pool. After a
hard day's work, the
pleasure of a midnight
swim... A luxurious
response to the
challenge of limited
space.

Plan of the three
levels.
Ground floor
1, 2, 3, 4. Study
areas
5. Toilet
6. Kitchen
7. Eating area
8. Staircase
9. Open air terrace
10. Garden
11. Swimming pool

Level 1
1. Bedroom
2. Bathroom
3. Bedroom
4. Staircase
5. Bedroom
6. Small sitting
room
7. Bedroom
8. Bedroom
9. Bathroom
10, 11. Toilets

Level 2
1. Living room
2. Kitchen
3. Open air terrace
4. Study area
5. Bedroom
6. Bathroom
7. Staircase

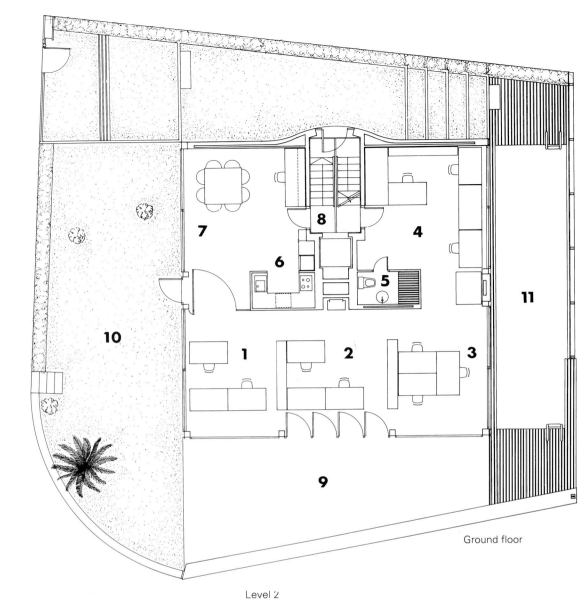

Ground floor

Level 1

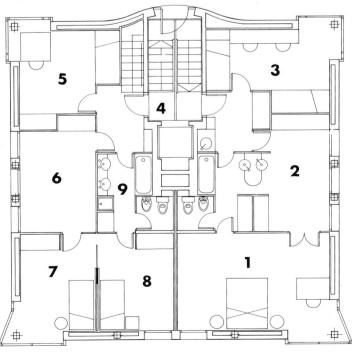

Level 2

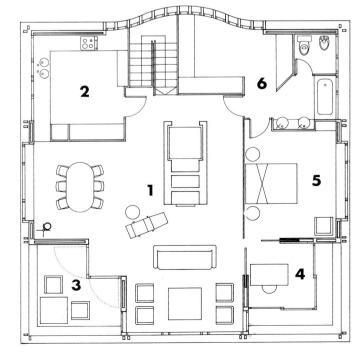

56 A house in Barcelona, Spain

Mount Tibidabo fairly bristles with residences that enjoy a panoramic view of the city and the sea. It is here that Beth Gali executed one of her latest projects.

On a square plan 12 meters by 12, the house has been placed in the middle of a small plot. The architect deploys an entire arsenal of heterogeneous materials, forms and textures, in a complex project that combines modernity and tradition. The facades superimpose three distinct registers, like strata that define the function of each level: offices on the first floor, bedrooms on the second, the third occupied for the most part by living spaces. The metallic structure, exposed on the ground and under the roof, allows one to guess the simplicity of the plan behind the complex outer shell. The building is structured around an elevator shaft that forms a well of light from above.

The ground floor looks like a glass cage open on the terrace and bordered on the east by a long narrow swimming pool, running along the very foot of the house. The inner volumes, entirely open, are an invitation to move freely from one office to another, to go out, breathe the air, feel the water. On the upper floor the facade becomes a protective shell against the sun. The thickness of the walls, tinted a Venetian green, retain the coolness in the bedrooms where light is dispensed only through narrow recessed windows and four larger angled windows, one at each corner.

Going against conventions, Beth Gali has crowned this modern edifice with a simple and traditional tile roof. Under the oblique angles of the beams, the volumes are set out with relation to the source of light, whether laterally or from above. The surrounding countryside blends with the warm colors of the wood, providing a rustic decor for the Le Corbusier or Macintosh furniture that suits it very well. In this vast open space loggias and quiet corners find their natural place. Rather than trying to seduce, Beth Gali enjoys multiplying experiences; rather than offering aesthetic perfection or imposing a particular style, she responds freely to the demands of everyday life.

At sundown, the polychrome facades give place to the magic of nocturnal contrasts, and the house seems to float on a cushion of light. □

A glazed opening in the center of the roof brings light from above into the upper floor, a space which is open and divided at the same time.

The exposed beams roofing covers the ocher colored bathroom.

In the loggia, the furniture, flooring and woodwork form an ensemble in perfect symbiosis with the wooded slopes of Mount Tibidabo.

The treatment of the tiles and the roofing both called upon traditional skills.

Opposite page
The living room is a vast space, fragmented into different areas where one can be alone. The sunlight is omnipresent.

Joan Rodón

A house in Barcelona, Spain

Broad colored surfaces on which lines are traced in wood and concrete, sometimes parallel, sometimes broken, to create a new space that is perfectly integrated in its natural setting.

The Serra de Collserola, at the outskirts of Barcelona, is one of those rare locations of the city that still boasts a natural environment. The towering pines on the rocky ground, the immense sky and the sea in the distance make it an exceptional site. Joan Rodón i Bonet knows the site perfectly. He was born in Barcelona and has lived here for over 42 years. In 1996 this house earned him a prize from the Eurobelgian Architectural Awards hailing "the quality, poetry and modernity of this realization in perfect respect of the landscape."

All you see of the house when you first arrive is the wooden trellis that lines the facade. The access is up a steep slope, where a succession of brightly-colored cubes seem to have been placed along the flank of the mountain. You climb a series of oblique stairways placed against the color-saturated walls. These cubes house various outbuildings — the garage, laundry-house and summer kitchen. As you pass diagonally by

the red, yellow and blue surfaces, then cross the stretches of green lawn, you feel as if you were mounting the steps of some immense staircase built for giants on the scale of the mountain itself.

The links woven by Joan Rodón with the city and the surrounding nature are the fruit of long intimacy. Reproducing in space what has grown with time, his architecture here takes the form of a voyage of initiation, whose virtues are contained in the simplicity of lines and distilled with the contact of the colors.

Invigorated by the climb, you discover the main building when you reach the summit, under the graceful silhouette of Norman Foster's Telecommunications Tower. Even here it offers itself to the eye partially masked behind blinds, which form a screen. This is adjustable to the amount of sunlight, for the sun strikes here due south. A projecting roof shields the entire length of the facade, keeping the heat at bay. After the verticals and diagonals of the ascension, the horizontals formed by the wooden slats are an invitation to rest or meditation, on one of the deck chairs on the terrace or in the living room in the shade of walls, zebra-striped by the strong light. Walls of cobalt blue create the illusion that the sky is part of the decor. A few sparse pieces of furniture dot the space – here a sofa with a low table, there a modern kitchen unit – while the colors on the walls repeat, in somewhat muted fashion, the same tones as the outer facades. The wood of the terraces, floors and facades is like an extension of the pines that cover the mountainside.

Inside, the empty space that doubles the height of the living room unites the top and bottom of the house, bringing the former into the field of vision of the latter. Along a wall, a staircase mounts to the upper floor. The volumes are arranged around a central L-shaped space, in which we find a study and a west-facing bedroom. Here, too, color structures the space and takes the place of furniture. On the second floor, another bedroom opening onto a terrace is like a balcony floating in the sky above Barcelona. □

The house consists of a succession of simple geometric shapes, linked together by stairways and built on a flank of the Collserola mountains.

Facing south, it wears a
protective screen,
made of the same
wood as the trees
among which it stands.
A large terrace extends
the living room, a cool
haven shielded from
the sun.

Yellow and blue
dominate the interior of
the house, as if to recall
the sun and sea that
stretch beyond
Barcelona to the
horizon.

A house near Barcelona, Spain

A summer sky with beating sun accentuates the warm colors of the walls and deepens the shadows around the windows, creating attractive contrasts.

Opposite page
A house characterized by its contrasts between straight lines and curves, open and closed spaces. Built into the portion of the cylinder separating the living room from the eating area is a barbecue facing the terrace.

Nestled in the mountains not far from Barcelona, the small Catalan town of Vacarisses has recently become a fashionable weekend getaway. Only a short distance from the industrial center of Terrassa and calm – far from the hubbub of the city – it is an attractive destination.

The architect Joan Carles Cardenal was fortunate to work with an enchanting terrain stretching over some 1,100 square meters (10,000 square feet) of luxuriant Mediterranean vegetation and gradually sloping southward, making for exceptional views to the east and west. His project aimed at satisfying his client's wishes in terms of the house's functional criteria while respecting the dominant characteristics of the site. Despite these constraints, the result is clearly a success. A distinctive structure of well-balanced curves and straight angles, its pink walls rising up in the middle of a rather traditional suburban setting, the house appears to be a subtle reference to the ubiquitous spirit of "movidad" or an indirect homage to the phantasmagoria of film maker Pedro Almadovar.

Built on a hillside, the house is comprised of two parallelepipeds of different size connected by a narrow glass-roofed passage running east-west. The rectilinear northern

70 A house near Barcelona, Spain

View of the east facade. The studied
interplay of small square openings
adds to the intimacy of this part of
the house, typically anchored in the
vernacular of traditional
Mediterranean design.

Opposite page
Frontal view of the glass corridor
connecting the two parts of the
house on the east facade. Its lines
divide up the landscape like a
Mondrian painting.

and southern facades are softened by two semi-cylindrical volumes arranged symmetrically opposite each other. A glass corridor crosses the house and joins the entry on the east side to an opening onto the western terrace. All indoor circulation is ordered around this central space in a truly contemporary re-appraisal of the traditional concept of the patio. The thick enclosing walls are pierced with small openings, except, of course, for the large door on the ground floor.

Each volume has its own function and is divided up vertically, the first being two stories high and the second only one. This second volume begins midway up the two floors of the first volume. One end comprises the "night" rooms, the other the "day" section.

One enters the house through the ground floor of the first volume which provides access to two bedrooms separated by a bathroom. This entrance area also leads directly to a terrace facing west. A staircase leads up to the half-level of the second volume shared by the dining room, kitchen and living room, all three generous, open spaces. Finally, at the very top, is the master bedroom, accessed from the living room up a daring metallic staircase.

The materials have been chosen for their quality and put in place with close attention down to the last detail: the outdoor aluminum window frames are painted in black satin; the interior walls have smooth stucco finishes; the doors and interior woodwork are covered in glossy varnish; floors are outlined by bands of tiles of different width; outdoor steel ramps and hand railings are painted in enamel.

In the characteristic spirit of Mediterranean traditional architecture, Cardenal has succeeded in formulating a peaceful and meditative environment through a resolutely contemporary design. □

Opposite page and below
A bold metal staircase with curved railings leading upstairs from the sitting room and elegantly spanning the void over the patio.

Above
The main entrance viewed from inside the atrium.

An astute correspondence
between interior and exterior
volumes. Here the living room
fireplace takes up the interior of
the half cylinder, its chimney
rising up beside that of the
barbecue on the north terrace
just behind.

The mezzanine sitting room with its metallic staircase which seems to leap up to the landing at mid-level. Here one sees the allusion to the relation between balcony, street and facade in an urban setting.

Josef Lackner

A house in Hatting, Austria

At night the house resembles an oven in which life and art fuse.

Opposite page
The entrance is through the "basement." The underside of the circular "umbrella" forming the upstairs quarters is clad in wooden shingles, setting an "ecological" tone to the ensemble.

While one is tempted to describe the Maier House in Hatting, Austria, as a flying saucer grounded in the mountains of Tyrol, this nonconformist house responds to a very specific set of circumstances.

The owner, a director of an art gallery, had a small terrain, a relatively limited budget and a preference for living in a wooden house. Entrusted with this project, Austrian architect Josef Lackner would prove more than capable of surmounting these initial minor difficulties.

To make the most of the very slight slope of the terrain, he dug out what would become the "basement," making for an area with multiple uses. The basic structure of the house is a mast encircled by a cone in what more or less resembles an Eskimo dwelling – or so it appears when viewed from the garden. This impression is underscored by the large overhang of the roof which, in places, is tangential to the natural slope. Seen from the other side, the area sculpted out on level with the ground lightens the perception of the construction as a whole, giving it the delicate appearance of a Japanese parasol.

To maximize the surface of the terrain, Lackner has ordered the bulk of the house vertically. The same economic and spatial considerations govern the interior layout as the total

On the larch wood
shingled roof these
original triangular
skylights light up even
the most private
rooms. At the very top,
under the mast, the
windows of the upper
mezzanine.

surface area does not exceed 120 square meters. While the rooms are set out according to their function and size, they are also designed to optimize the natural light.

The house is comprised of three levels including the basement, which serves as the entrance. Here, from the hallway, a central staircase leads up to the living areas. Where certain rooms have compatible uses they are treated as one volume, as for example the kitchen and living room. In this way, despite being individually small, the ensemble gives the illusion of space.

The stairwell crowned by a small glass rotunda and integrated into the general layout gives the feeling of an art gallery in the heart of the home. Its paintings hung throughout add their unique presence to the interior atmosphere. The living/dining room with its continuous glass partition wall is the most open space, interrupted only by the fireplace. Facing south, it opens out generously to the garden, with a view that gives it all its charm.

For technical reasons, the walls are made of modular panels set at an angle. Wood dominates in this house with its ceilings in plywood and roof lined in larch wood, a contrast with the large glass windows that surround the house. In response to the harsh climate, the floors are all carpeted to add much-needed warmth.

Josef Lackner has succeeded in building a highly original construction despite the material constraints inherent in the project. A surprising sight amidst a conformist, picture-perfect neighborhood, the house is, nevertheless, in perfect symbiosis with its natural surroundings. □

The "umbrella" structure not only lightens the whole visually, it also opens up more space on the ground and extends the protected area of the garden.

The living room entirely lined with windows sets up a closer relationship with the garden. The white block of the fireplace creates a striking contrast with the predominant glass and wood of this construction.

80 A house in Hatting, Austria

The mezzanine seen from the living room. Contrasting materials – wood, rough concrete, glass and plaster – highlight the display of the artworks.

Opposite page
The shaded terrace in the lower part of the garden. The ribbed underside of the upper floor makes the analogy with a Japanese parasol even more appropriate.

The glass expanses between the beams light up the living room tucked in below the mezzanine.

Alessandro Mendini

A house on Lake Orta, Italy

This project originated in 1980 when Alberto Alessi, the famous "couturier of kitchenware and dining," asked his friend the Milanese architect Alessandro Mendini to plan the design for a villa on the shores of lake Orta in what would become, eight years later, the "House of Happiness."

In the words of its creator, "the various buildings taken as a whole are like a small fortified village, complete with narrow streets, steps and small squares, spread out over a thin strip of land bordering the lake. The different "houses" of this village correspond to the rooms that make up a home. Each one, whether created or already in place, is defined by a particular feature and color, with its own unique material. They combine old and modern in the same spontaneous way a village is formed, or in the spirit of accretion of the Acropolis."

Visitors must resign themselves to a fragmented view of the ensemble, as the property unfolds progressively, revealing its continuity much like a novel, a string of subtle interactions between interior and exterior, a labyrinth that leads to simple yet surprising places. Its polymorphic appearance is underscored by the various creations of its prestigious collaborators: Aldo Rossi, Ettore Sottsass, Frank O. Gehry and Roberto Venturi.

The surrounding wall is comprised of two long sections: a dry stone traditional wall and a concrete partition encrusted with Murano glass. The entrance portico by Milton Glaser takes up local tradition with its wrought iron crown. An S-shaped staircase first leads us from street level to the gardens with their gravel pathways and alternate stone and mosaic

Opposite page
The loggia's curved wall provides a skillful transition between the living quarters, the gymnasium and the library.

A pale-colored concrete wall encrusted with Murano glass surrounds the main buildings that make up this "miniature village." The House of Happiness is characterized by its diversity of styles.

One of the main characteristics of the House of Happiness is its diversity of styles

paving, flower beds, vegetable gardens, vines, badminton courts, a small greenhouse, gazebos, fountains and galleries – without forgetting, of course, the pool with its mosaic floral design. The vegetation provides a luxuriant backdrop, drawing the eye to the gardens, the lake and the sky.

We then reach the terrace of a small limestone temple, which acts as the principal entry to the house and, as it holds the stairwell, as the focus of the horizontal and vertical movement of the whole property.

In the first main building we find the dining room and the kitchen on the ground floor, with two bedrooms on the upper level. This is the outcome of the skillful restoration of a 16th-century farm with a few additions dating from the 18th-century. A fresco on one of its walls depicts "Our Lady of the Path." The fireplace in the living room has a circular steel enameled hood, signed Achille Castiglioni. As for the kitchen – its importance to the Alessi family goes without saying – it has been conceived of as a laboratory, professionally fitted out with high-precision equipment and furniture. The copper roof

The swimming pool is the central piece in the layout of the gardens. In the immediate background is the eccentric lookout tower by Aldo Rossi, standing beside a rotunda commanding views over lake Orta and the surrounding mountains.

This pergola is resolutely Italian – a traditional and harmonious image of the House of Happiness.

The rustic facade of this stone guest house is a testimony to the original state of the building.

The strict geometric composition of these elements is softened by the delicate tones and refined juxtaposition of materials.

A classical symmetry and a polished travertine finish give the entry of the house its air of a small temple.

has three chimneys designed by Riccardo Dalisi, featuring the ram, Aries, and two doves.

From here we enter the two-story high library – like a mirror of Alberto Alessi's memory – in what used to be a 16th-century hayloft. It has been designed by Roberto Venturi based on the classical model: walls entirely covered in books and shelves, countertops by the windows, ladders and secret panels. The woodwork is painted in light tones of yellow, red, blue and white.

In the loggia we discover a room of rustic appearance, characterized by a series of galleries. The walls are painted in green tones with frescos in floral designs; in Palladian style, the floor has a multicolored marble mosaic; the fireplace, designed by Ettore Sottsass, has a conically-shaped, laminated steel hood; and the flat roof is decorated with an ocher dome in enamel.

What remains of the original building transformed into a guest house is a stone facade; its side walls are modern, clad in plaster with a lacquered black aluminum roof.

A little further along we come to the gymnasium in true 1950's style with a framework of wooden beams covered in tiles and supported by four solid granite pillars. Upstairs is the gym proper with, downstairs, a sauna, Jacuzzi and portico.

Below the guest house, in the middle of the orchard is a small greenhouse, the imaginative contribution of Frank O. Gehry. Opposite, like a proto-industrialist vestige, stands the lookout post designed by Aldo Rossi, a steel cylinder encircled by an outdoor staircase and capped with a small brick cone. With the adjoining domed rotunda, they stand in the same axis as the swimming pool and, of course, the kitchen.

In the words of its owner, the "House of Happiness" has become the "House of Happy Designs. Happy because they are well planned, authentic and free, conceived along the lines that freedom is essential to all design that aims to be a work of art." □

The circular facade of the loggia, punctuated with narrow arches and painted with a fresco in almond green.

The large living room and fireplace center piece by Ettore Sottsass with its laminated steel hood. The room is lit up by a dome skylight.

Opposite page
The gymnasium's wooden framework and its hardwood floor create a warm atmosphere, ideal for relaxation... and exercise!

A house in Loco, Switzerland

The pathway with its black steel railings and the suspended box forming the entrance porch.

Opposite page
The three main levels built into the steep mountainside. Here one sees the rhythmic alternation between mass and emptiness on the facades.

There are more than one ways to approach the delicate issue of integrating a house within its site. Some architects, Cristian Cirici for one, opt for an altogether vernacular solution, reusing the shapes of the past, often keeping their original form intact, at least on the exterior; then there are those like the Tessin architect Luigi Snozzi who start out from a wholly opposite standpoint.

Snozzi sees the urban house as an archetype, the city as dwelling being, in his opinion, a true concept of freedom. Expressing himself through what could be termed a "classic modernity," his material of predilection being rough-hewn concrete, the relationship he develops with the natural surroundings is far from nostalgic. His transformations are in fact "humbly" modern. Snozzi's constructions draw extensively from the region's particular traditions or culture, as well as from the morphology of the landscape and the skills of the local population. These elements are then projected as a whole into present-day reality.

This one-family house in the Onsernone valley is a fine illustration. Set amidst vines planted in terraces up a steep climb, the house dominates a large valley in the Loco region on a site that will undoubtedly see significant development in the near future.

Viewed from the outside, the house appears as a concrete

Viewed from the west,
the facade of the
Walser House is in
intimate dialogue with
the neighboring
traditional houses in the
distance.

Opposite page
The living room,
inundated with light,
opens out into a terrace
overlooking the valley.

cube solidly implanted on the hillside and spreading out over three terraces. Its curious slate roof in the shape of a four-sided pyramid is a concession, as it were, to the local style in practice since the 18th-century. Because of well-enforced urban planning regulations strictly prohibiting any leveling out of the terrain or the use of land fills, the two lower levels of the house are built into the mountainside itself, a feature that makes for its very particular layout.

In the north-south axis of the slope and viewed from the side, this eight-meter wide parallelepiped offers a largely buried northern facade – indeed, the main entrance is the only opening on this side. The south facade, in contrast, spreads out over three levels, majestically dominating the valley below. A recurrent feature of Snozzi's designs, a pergola stands at the far eastern end of the terrain, serving as a gazebo or eating area in the summer months. A narrow alley, bordered by a low parapet, connects it to the main house. Similarly, the path to the main entrance inscribes a line along the edge of the vineyard, taking up the profile of the

A semicircular expanse creates a continuity between the interior and exterior, transforming the dining room into a rotunda with a full view of the landscape.

The white marble fireplace and granite table echo off each other.

landscape. Together these structures form the dominant horizontal of the composition and ensure its perfect integration within the relief of the terraces.

Entering the house, the visitor passes into a large area arranged like a gangway around an empty center, covered by a cupola formed by the underside of the pyramid-shaped roof. In addition to the entrance hallway, this gallery holds a nook for dining in one corner and a study in another. Its three circular windows provide special views from each main area. This cozy volume, much like a cruise ship, overhangs a very different style of room that opens to the exterior. Leading down to this area and set against the back wall built into the hillside is a white staircase ramp with black wooden handrails. Here there is a more "social" atmosphere, and while it appears to serve merely as a kitchen/dining room, the area reveals a much wider, congenial use with its white marble fireplace built into the wall where the family can gather round or entertain. In this sense, the house preserves the vestiges of the layout of a rural house. Its south-facing facade has a semicircular glass wall that gives out onto an open terrace, itself turned out to face three directions, making for exceptional views of the surroundings and setting up a contrast with the upper, more closed level.

The terrace clearly corresponds to the horizontal gap in the main facade. Leading away from the terrace to the pergola is a flagstone path. Returning indoors, a staircase to the basement takes us to the "hold," the night area where four bedrooms and their adjoining bathrooms are distributed over two levels. Here again, depending on one's tastes and mood, the spartan atmosphere recalls a monk's cell or a transatlantic cabin. The three small windows on the south facade belong to these rooms.

The interior is characterized by its uniformity and its dominant tones of black and white. Its geometric volumes are tempered by the light through their openings and the dining room's expanse of glass. The atmosphere owes as much to a stunning landscape as it does to the light and shadow cast on bright white walls. This is an interior for a purist, a design that would surely have met with the approval of a certain Charles-Edouard Jeanneret-Le Corbusier.

The Walser House is a resolutely modern design, yet fully in tune with the particularities of its site, a home with a special penchant for relaxation and introspection. □

General plan
1. Living room
2. Kitchen
3. Toilet
4. Fireplace
5. Open air terrace
6. Pathway
7. Pergola

Cross-section
1. Upper level : entrance - sitting room - study
2. Terrace level : living-room - kitchen - open air terrace (see General Plan)
3. Lower level 1 : two bedrooms - bathroom
4. Lower level 2 : two bedrooms - bathroom

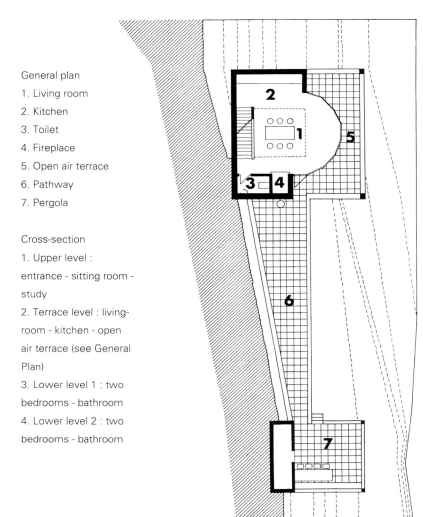

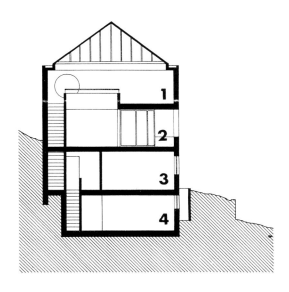

Upstairs, a small sitting room and a study
area with their respective porthole
window.

Opposite page
A bird's-eye view of the kitchen/dining
room. This perspective gives an idea of
the different atmosphere and lighting
found on each level.

Peter Lorenz

A house in Innsbruck, Austria

Viewed at night, the
Gasser House takes on
the magical
atmosphere of the
Tyrol winter...

Opposite page
The Gasser House
delicately blends into a
landscape of silver
birches and its dark
backdrop of pines.
Such refinement has a
Japanese air, and yet
the picture could not be
more typically Austrian.

This vast clearing on a hilltop, surrounded on all sides by
dark pines and snow-capped trees, is a landscape fit for the
setting of Lucchino Visconti's film "Ludwig." Rising out of the
trees, this neo-classical temple with pale yellow facades and
accents of white is something of a wayward testimony to the
most prestigious of Austro-Hungarian traditions. Reaching into
the distance, a curious wooden pontoon painted white
provides a passage, as it were, to the strange tales of olden
times...

We are in fact in Innsbruck, in the heart of the Tyrol. This
house, built in the early 19th-century by a rich family of
Viennese aristocrats used to be a rustic retreat. On the edge
of ruin, it laid abandoned for years before its new owners
entrusted its restoration to Peter Lorenz in 1984. Lorenz is a
figurehead of the Austrian "New Wave." In order to protect
the environment, the Austrian government has made it illegal
to build new constructions on the outskirts of certain large
cities; in this particular case, the project received the go ahead
only because it involved the restoration of a pre-existing
structure. Lorenz decided to play the game: he would respect
the original spirit of the place but by employing the most
innovative architectural solutions. His projects always prove to

Plan of the attic
1. Game room - library
2. Balcony
3. Open air terrace

The upstairs floor plan
1. Bedroom
2. Dressing room
3. Bathroom
4. Bedroom
5. Bedroom
6. Bedroom
7. Bedroom
8. Open air terrace

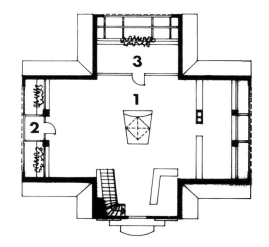

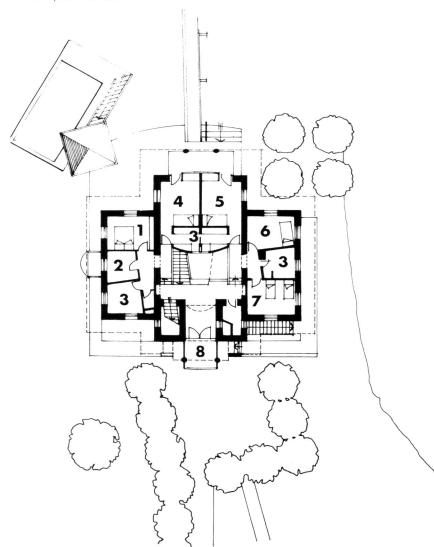

be coherent from the point of view of their relationship to their natural setting, and he is quick to engender the appropriate shapes and colors to achieve the right symbiosis with the site. Here, the creamy yellow and white blend beautifully into this snowy picture, with only a few thin metal structures in bright blue adding their accents – in anticipation, perhaps, of a summer sky.

From the outset some changes needed to be made to the infrastructure as a whole. In order to make a crawl space and prevent dampness from rising up through the house, the floorboards were raised and a platform built around the house, thus creating an overall improvement to its foundation. An interior lining, 12 centimeters (5 inches) thick, of assorted bricks was added behind the original masonry to form an air shaft for better thermal insulation. This extra thickness of the walls made for more leeway in creating interesting openings.

Besides the peristyles on its two facades, the resolutely neo-classic element to the house is underscored by the long wooden passage of the pontoon crossing the terrain where it dips down slightly behind the villa on the west side. In the summer, this dip forms a small lake, no doubt picturesque with its swans and water lilies. Creating a true link between the building and nature, this poetic aerial bridge connects the living room to the end of the grounds.

Built on a square-shaped site, the house originally followed a cross-shaped plan with two stories and an attic – a frequent layout in the Renaissance, and notably that of Palladio's famous villa "the Rotonde."

Each facade comprises three volumes: two lateral wings with two windows, one above the other, set far back in the wall to shelter them from the wind and cold, and finally a large central section projecting forward. This projection on the main facade forms a porch framed by two pillars to the main entry, continued on the upper level as a slightly rounded balcony open to the upper gallery of the living room. The ensemble is crowned by a majestic arch built into the pediment of the attic.

This direct Palladian reference on the exterior is repeated on the interior. Crossing the doorstep, one enters a vast, high-ceilinged living room. This area articulates the smaller rooms that fan out from the central staircase, a layout prompted as much by an esthetic concern as by an effort not to alter the supporting partition walls. This main area, open onto the western facade and the passageway crossing the lake, has a mezzanine on the other side overlooking the balcony of the porch and providing a unique view of the forest (an ideal spot

The south facade: pale yellow and white are in perfect harmony with this snowy scene in black and white. A long white pontoon extends from the living room all the way to the far end of the grounds.

102 A house in Innsbruck, Austria

for intimate secrets). The north side forms a little nook or fireplace corner set further back, and another intimate area with the kitchen/dining room composite. The interior is bathed in natural light and the furnishing is soft and sober: leather couches in the living room, light cushions in the fireplace corner, ocher floors with venetian terra cotta flagstones. The beige walls are coated in waxed plaster. Opposite the staircase, a large fresco by Wolfgang Seltner of the plans of the house adds its colorful touch and sets the atmosphere. As for the rest, furniture, curtains and Tibetan woolen carpets complete the harmony of natural tones and colors.

The kitchen/eating area alone takes up a third of the ground floor. Its open layout is characteristic of northern countries. Warm tones of blond wood chairs, tables and cupboards predominate. Other typical details of the traditional Austrian kitchen are its small square windows, its wooden stove separating the two areas, and its green patterned seat covers.

Upstairs are five bedrooms with closets and bathrooms in two units. The first unit is accessed from the landing; the other contains the master bedroom. The bedrooms have thick gray carpets with apricot-colored closets and cotton curtains adding their touch of brightness.

The last floor – the attic – offers a surprise: a magic space with a wooden framework visible above. This is at once a game room, a loggia, a library and a place where the household can gather. This vast room is in fact a second sitting room.

In this exemplary restoration, Peter Lorenz has once again succeeded in forming an authentic dialogue between the architecture and the landscape. Furthermore, he has kept the elegance of this stately dwelling intact while adapting it to the requirements of modern life. There are plans for an extension to build a ski school on the property: our guess is that the influx of people will not bother its proud occupants, themselves fanatics of the sport. □

A large arched picture window built into the pediment of the attic outlines a breathtaking view of the distant mountains and sets us dreaming...

Opposite page
The balcony's metallic structures built into the entrance peristyle. Not only do they add a touch of bright color to the ensemble, they are rooted in a tradition dating back to the Middle Ages, brilliantly illustrated in the not so distant 18th-century in Austria by the pioneers of Art Nouveau (Otto Wagner, Josef Hoffman, Koloman Mosser).

This all-white
atmosphere is
interrupted by the red
and yellow lines of the
light fixtures, with the
discrete echo of the
curtain's frame.

A detail of the lower
arcature of the perimeter
with plants growing in the
window sill, creating a
subtle transition between
the interior's cozy
atmosphere and the
omnipresent nature.

Martin Wagner

A house in Sessa, Switzerland

A wayward hiker stumbling upon this curious edifice in the green mountain tops of Mount Bigorio might well wonder whether he was hallucinating, so striking is this entanglement of glass, steel and concrete – half sugar refinery, half industrial shed.

An architect's stylistic choices are often conditioned by topographical and geographical constraints, or else they stem from purely cultural and historical elements. They may equally spring from the ideology of a particular period, as in the case of the constructions that came out of the Rationalist School in the inter-war period or as in the late 1970's and early 1980's, when many of the constructions reflected a certain confidence in the wonders of technology and the paradoxical growth in ecological awareness that prompted much research in alternative energy systems, in the hope of reaching a symbiosis between man and nature.

These "fruitful" utopias are undoubtedly what spurred Basel architect Martin Wagner to draw up the plans for this house in the Tessin. Set on a hill in the Beredino region among lush vegetation, the house is comprised of three parts: a main building – the house proper –, a central greenhouse for a winter garden, and a guest house. The predominant materials are glass, steel and rough-hewn concrete. The

Opposite page

The sculptural aspect of parts of this house is accentuated by the colorful touch of its metal window frames and handrails.

A structure in three parts: the house proper to the left, the winter garden in the center and the guest house to the right.

The winter garden forms the kernel of the house and connects the guest rooms to the main quarters. It also forms an extension of the natural surroundings, bringing nature indoors through its glass panels.

Opposite page
The interior, like the exterior, plays on the opposition of mineral elements and metal painted in primary colors.

A cross-section of the house reveals the workings of the solar panels in relation to the different angles of the sun.

ensemble, much like a massive hi-tech sculpture, resplendent against the bright Tessin sky, is here and there highlighted with a touch of cobalt blue or the bright red of its woodwork and railings.

The overall construction is conceived as a thermic trap: a large glass structure faces south-south-west and a compact unit encloses the three remaining sides. The general floor plan reinforces the initial concept: the interior with its capacity to capture and store solar energy; the solar panels of the roof; and the glass of the interior garden, which joins the various parts of the house.

The main entrance, located on the lower level, is accessed through the greenhouse. Through the back facade, a secondary entrance provides for a private access to the upstairs bedrooms, ensuring greater independence from the communal living areas. The greenhouse is used all year round and holds an open fireplace, the heat from which is, of course, recycled along with the heat generated by the concrete base of the roof terrace and the terra cotta floors. The adjoining living room, at the center of the floor plan, is flooded with light all day long streaming in through the large curved glass windows at the rear of the solar panel. The altogether sparse furniture lets the red terra cotta tiles and the view stretching as far as the blue line of the Alps set the atmosphere. The inside wall surrounding the back of the room is lined with bricks painted in white. A concrete fireplace topped by a simple round metal tube juts forward in the middle of the glass facade. Chrome-framed armchairs covered in natural canvas surround the fireplace – witnesses of an already legendary period... A little further along stands the dining room table, lit up by a recessed lighting built into the ceiling. Built behind the winter garden, the kitchen overlooks the living room.

In addition to the entry mentioned above, a double flight of stairs, beginning where the dining area extends into the living room, leads to the upstairs bedrooms aligned with the facade, their wash rooms in the back. Set on either side of the glass opening, light can thus penetrate through to the lower level.

Often cited with admiration but seldom (or badly) copied, this solar construction has been the object of controversy as to its true viability. It remains, nevertheless, a bench work in the history of solar construction. □

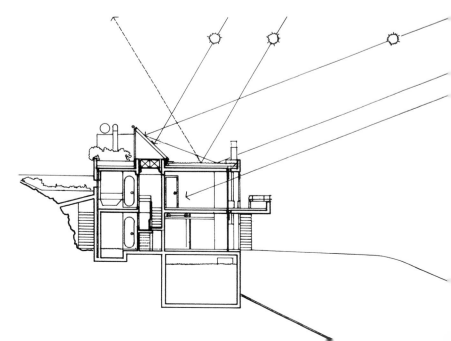

The dining table is lit up by the opening in the ceiling where the wires of the hanging lamps add
"irregularity" to this interior of straight lines.

Opposite page
In the winter garden both the plants and the occupants can enjoy abundant light all year round. In the
winter, this imposing double fireplace, which also gives onto the guest's quarters, heats the house.

Following pages
Around the fireplace, through the large windows and beyond the sculptural delight of the staircase, the
view stretches far and wide across the valley.

Manfred Kovatsch

A house on the Ossiacher Lake, Austria

A subtle contrast of colors comes alive in the sunlight: the golden hues of the facade's wooden slats and interplay of small openings, the gray of the long roof and the peaceful green of the vegetation.

Opposite page
The house evokes a ship's prow ploughing ahead.

Every boy's dream is to build a log cabin at the bottom of a secret garden. Undoubtedly such a childhood fantasy is what spurred Austrian architect Manfred Kovatsch to build this eccentric house in 1977.

A thirty minute drive from the town of Villash in southern Austria, the house was originally intended as a secondary residence. Perched some 350 meters above Ossiacher Lake on a steep terrain sloping down to the water's edge, the house gives its occupants a panoramic view over the landscape.

Like different decks on a ship, the rectilinear floor plan is composed of four interwoven levels supported by a wooden framework. The four parallel porticos making up this structure are each joined and braced by cross beams, forming the shape of a St. Andrews cross. Inside are three staircases of different heights, two of which connect the three floors in the back and a third serving the frontal section and leading to the lower levels of the living room and the lower platform.

To make the most of the very steep inclination of the site, a large floor, built between the first two porticos and crossing over the slope, provides a much-appreciated sun deck in the

This side view has a distinct mountain
feel to it – a true chalet, complete with
a long log fence and its simple opening
to the main entrance.

summer and a place to store wood for the winter months. A wooden ladder set at an angle connects this floor to the second level where we find the living room and the main adjoining terrace. In the corner of the terrace is a curious triangular cabin, its base set at a 45° angle from the edge of the floor. Lined entirely with windows and crowned by a pointed roof, this gazebo offers superb views over the lake and the mountains.

Inside the living room, a lateral staircase leads up to the dining room and the kitchen both of which share the third level. The dining room floor juts out above the living room and partially hangs in the empty space. Up an open staircase, a bedroom with four beds is nestled under the attic roof. In fact, this is more than a bedroom; it has multiple uses with, in the center of the floor, a built-in bath tub and two Plexiglas washbasins in among its exposed tubing – a family bathroom as it were.

The actual facade is comprised of four square glass panels with diagonal crosspieces. The two lower panels, belonging to the living room, slide along metal rods that jut out on either side. When closed, their diagonal crosspieces align with the upper panels to form a St. Andrew's cross. This transparent design gives the house its visibility and optimizes the light.

The straight-forward simplicity of this structure, based on basic principles of construction, enabled the architect to assemble the skeleton in a matter of days. After the stairs were firmly attached, the walls and roof were added. The very elongated shape of this chalet is what gives it its strong character and adds to its "visible anchoring" in the landscape. A triple outer layer of wood and sheet metal and the steeply perched roof protect the inner nest of the home. The changing color of the roof from bright silver in the sunlight to mother of pearl in bad weather resonates with symbolic meaning.

The pale yellow and golden brown tones of the beams in larch wood and the spruce planks of the framework stand out from the surrounding dark green forests and meadows. The architect's particular choice of wood was not only influenced by its local use, which makes it immediately available, larch wood is especially resilient to extreme climatic variations and spruce is ideal for sheltered areas. The indoor walls are entirely lined in satin-like wood paneling, while the six centimeters between the interior wall and the outside cladding are filled with fiberglass wool for insulation.

The lateral facades have small openings that,

The house is beautifully integrated into an emerald landscape, the solid silver line of its roof protecting an intricate mesh of beams below.

An intriguing stove, like
a little train, joins in this
symphony of lines,
from the wooden floor
boards, the balustrades
and the graceful
latticework on either
side of this large
verandah.

This enchanting view
over the lake and the
mountain, and the bold
lines of the supporting
beams make up the
principal furnishings of
the sitting room.

nevertheless, create interesting and varied views of the landscape. Grouped together or alone, these openings give a rhythm to this otherwise unified wooden surface.

Manfred Kovatsch's construction reconciles practicality with a visually appealing design. But this is more than just a welcoming mountain refuge; it is also an exhilarating home perched on the "edge of danger," a home in which its occupants live out each moment with intensity. □

This is the stunning view from the bedroom tucked under the never-ending roof which protects the verandah.

The terrace on the lower level is clearly an ideal spot for relaxing – the hammock and bathtub are no coincidence...

Opposite page
Like a spider web, this structure perched on the edge of the verandah is ideal for daydreaming; looking down over the lake time stands still.

The sensation of heights is present at all times even when dining.

Here, the compact space, exposed tubing, hanging utensils, an eating area that like a cabin evokes the feeling of being on a boat.

Opposite page
A bedroom with an air of a dormitory. The odd tubular sculpture in the middle of the floor is in fact a bathtub built into the floor, topped by two Plexiglas wash basins.

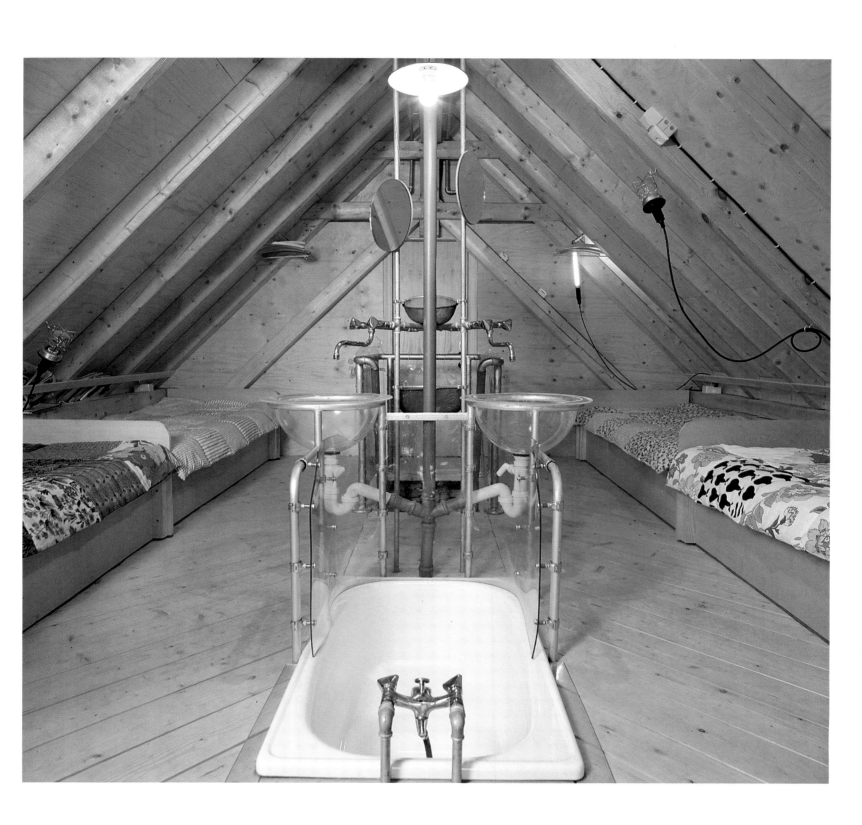

Franco and Paolo Moro

A house in Gordola, Switzerland

With its elegant arched metal pergola and its splendid view, this terrace is both a solarium and belvedere.

Opposite page
Built near a mountain range, the Matter House is a gray cube with paired down lines rising up out of a vineyard.

The history of art has shown time and again that the most outstanding works of art are those that, at first sight, strike us with their simplicity. The Matter House project by architects Paolo and Franco Moro proves the significance of this adage.

Some of the initial constraints, a sloping terrain where an old alluvial river bed crosses a local service road and high tension wires, confined the house to the lowest portion of the site. We should not, however, overlook the site's magnificent, unobstructed view of the surrounding mountains, much like being on the stage of a Greek amphitheater. We are in Gordola, an enclave forming a small Tessin ski station at the northern point of the Lago Maggiore.

Two distinctive elements immediately come to view: a three-stories high cube of gray breeze blocks topped by a curved roof and, opposite, a well-defined parallelepiped structure. Half-buried, this last structure encloses the garage and holds the swimming pool on its upper level. A garden with a strict geometric layout and outlined by low hedges separates the two buildings, with the local road on one side and an adjoining vegetable garden on the other.

Let us take a closer look, giving special attention to the four sides of this intriguing cube, which is reminiscent of the

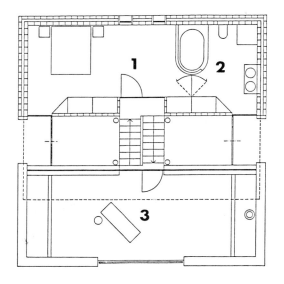

Opposite page

In the back, the sunken garage with a swimming pool built into its roof where a private enclosure protects its from onlookers.

Plan of the 2nd floor.

1. Bedroom
2. Bathroom
3. Solarium/terrace

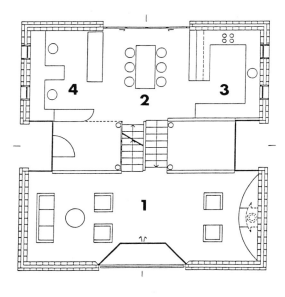

Plan of the 1st floor.

1. Living room
2. Dining room
3. Kitchen
4. Study area

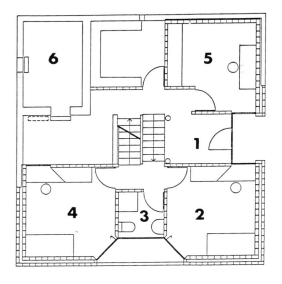

Plan of the ground floor.

1. Entrance
2. Bedroom
3. Shower-room
4. Bedroom
5. Bedroom
6. Study
7. Game room

martial style of military outposts that dot the landscape of the Aosta valley.

The entrance facade to the north is the most austere: a perfect rectangle with a single door and two circular windows above. The wall of the facade is cut down the middle vertically by a narrow window taking up the full height of the building, the glass surface being set further back from the bare exterior wall. The first half of both the eastern and western facades is brought alive by two circular windows, similar to those on the front side. A flight of steps leads to the lower part. On the south side, the house opens out to the garden and view of the surrounding mountains. A square set in the center forms a large picture window taking up the two upper levels, and a series of five circular windows punctuates its lower level. The top of the edifice is crowned by a curved corrugated iron structure along three quarters of its length, the remaining area forming a south-facing terrace with a thin metallic structure above.

The interior layout is a perfect echo of the exterior envelope. The two gaps in the lateral facades form a central shaft (this layout articulated around a central space with glass sides recalls the treatment of the house in Vacarisses by Joan Carles Cardenal). This shaft forms the true heart of the house and orchestrates all the other rooms. It also provides a source of abundant natural light, giving the house its warm atmosphere. It encloses a concrete staircase contained within four cylindrical steel pillars and outlined with slender steel railings. The shaft literally springs up out of the depths of the ground toward the upper levels and the terrace. Here and there the varied heights of the floors can be seen. With glass on two of its sides, the staircase is also visible from the outside. Upstairs we come to three bedrooms and a restroom, followed by the kitchen/living/dining area, the master bedroom and its adjoining bathroom and, at last, the panoramic solarium.

The daytime areas open directly onto the empty center and staircase, recreating the city feeling of looking down from a balcony onto the street.

Beyond its successful symbiosis of practicality with esthetics, the Matter House is a fine example of the contemporary Tessin school of architecture, elsewhere intelligently illustrated by such individuals as Mario Botta.◻

The north facade. In
line with the house,
this granite table is in
full shade by midday,
making for a perfect
outdoor dining area in
the summer.

128 A house in Gordola, Switzerland

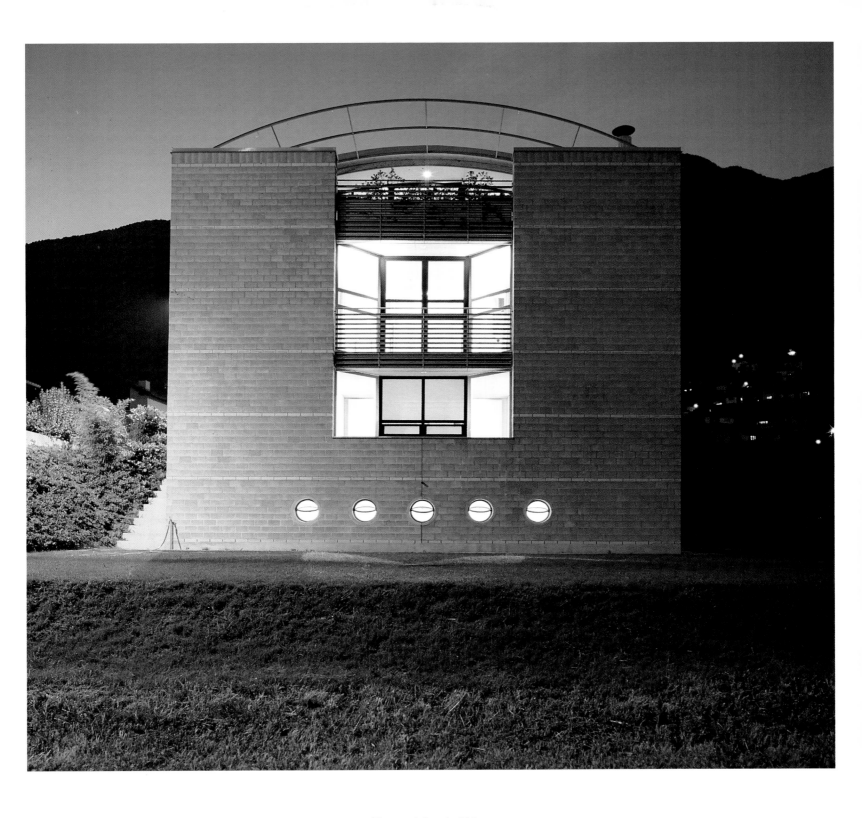

The south facade. This
night view highlights
the studied interplay of
material and
emptiness. It magnifies
the large central
window and the lower
strip of porthole
windows.

The kitchen and dining room
form one large and open space
with direct access onto a
central patio. The only
separation between the two is
a free-standing countertop.

Opposite page
The open staircase with the
diagonal lines of its railings
adds lightness to the interior.

Erich Schneider-Wessling

A house in Aachen, Germany

The side of this house facing away from the forest toward a meadow offers up a complex and fragmentary facade.

Opposite page
A brick path of steps separating the "children's wing" from the rest of the house leads to the discrete main entrance.

Aachen was one of Carolus Magnus's favorite places and the birthplace of Mies Van der Rohe. Since World War II, the town has been surrounded by parkland, making for ideal sites for architectural projects.

It was on one of these natural sites, halfway between forest and meadows, that Erich Schneider-Wessling chose to build this house for a couple and their four children. With the forest to the north, the edifice faces the meadows with its complex facade, forming two distinct wings on either side of a triangular section projected forward. Its walls clad in wooden slats and its angled roofs stretching all the way down to the ground evoke the traditional architecture of chalets. Yet its sharp angles pointing up through the leafy oaks and its fragmented volumes, belong to an altogether contemporary design, far from such traditional models.

Erich Schneider-Wessling's primary aim was to provide his clients with a home well adapted to their needs. He has combined their concern for comfort with a home that incorporates nature and exploits the daylight hours, optimizing the sunlight.

This is an architecture that lends itself to multiple levels and expresses itself through the fragmentation of its facades and roofs, with a succession of volumes either recessed or

To the south-east is a
succession of terraces
and pergolas. The
triangular volume in the
far end contains a
sauna.

Opposite page
Water is a central
element of the house in
the summer. Here is
where the family
gathers for meals and
to cool off.

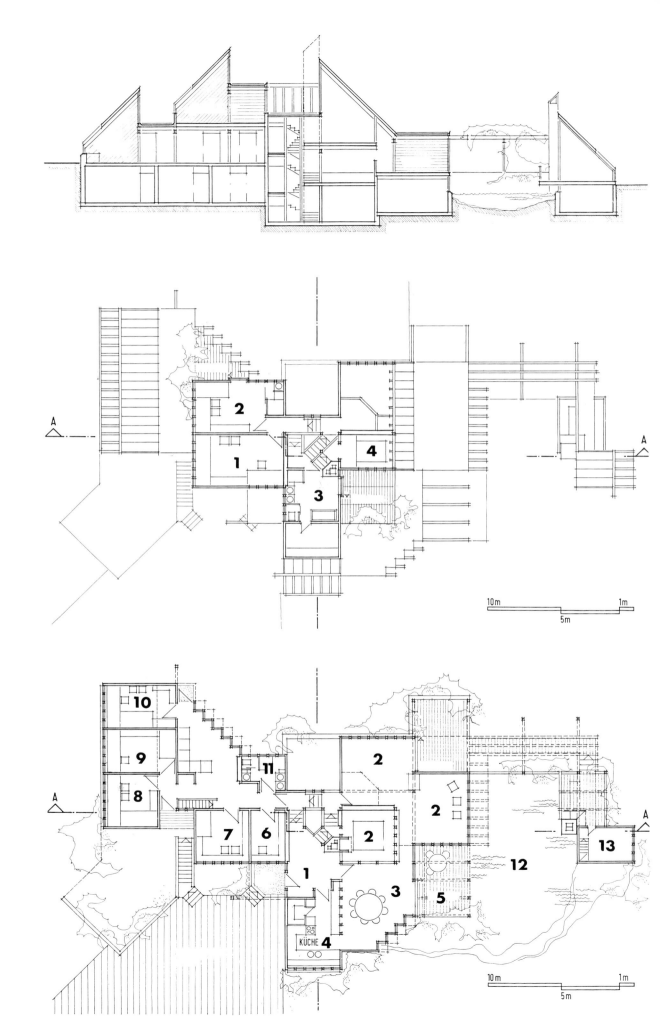

Elevation floor plan;
plan of the first floor;
plan of the ground
floor. These plans
reveal the complexity
of the volumes as well
as their numerous
different levels.
The square living room
is at the center of this
mesh of rooms.

Plan of the ground floor
1. Entrance
2. Living room
3. Dining room
4. Kitchen
5. Open air terrace
6. Bedroom
7. Bedroom
8. Bedroom
9. Bedroom
10. Bedroom
11. Bathroom
12. Pond
13. Sauna

Plan of the first floor
1. Bedroom
2. Bedroom
3. Bathroom
4. Study/Studio

Opposite page
The wooden slats
enclosing the windows
extend to form a
pergola over the
terrace.

Larch wood
predominates both
inside and out, forming
the main structure and
lining the roof, floors,
walls and ceilings.

jutting forward. The functions of each space are, nevertheless, clearly defined. The main entrance is accessed by a staircase located on the west side, the area reserved for the bedrooms. A brick wall following the steps separates the children's quarters from the rest of the house. The east wing, conceived as much for indoors as for outdoors living, has a long U-shaped band with pergolas and terraces surrounding a pond and ending in a sauna. This forest of posts defines a large intermediary space – between a park and a living area – and allows the water to come all the way up to the sitting room.

The fireplace is clearly the center of the house. The dining room, library and other small sitting rooms open out onto this central point, while maintaining a certain independence. With their different gathering points, these convivial areas form an ensemble; visually a whole, however, they take up different levels. Each area is conducive to taking meals, whether indoors or outdoors, on the verandah or on the west-facing terrace to enjoy the sunset.

While wood dominates on the exterior, brick plays an equally important role, imparting a sober warmth to the interior where it forms the walls and floors. Glass also adds its music to this rustic symphony, providing views over the towering trees to the north, the meadows to the south, and the water to the east. Forming narrow bands along the height of the walls, in large expanses, or in angles on its roof, glass gives this home its air of a prism, cut to receive light all day and all year round. □

While these interior
volumes display
generous open spaces,
they are, nevertheless,
fragmented by wooden
posts and changes in
level. The sitting room
around the fireplace,
the library and the
dining room form an
ensemble while each
area keeps a certain
independence.

Jan Van Tellingen

A house in Gendt, The Netherlands

Deeply inspired by 1930's design, hidden behind this high brick wall are two work spaces echoing the same contrast between openness and opacity that characterizes the main house.

Located on the outskirts of the small town of Gendt, Holland, this house sits on the edge of open country with a view over the fields stretching as far as the eye can see, interrupted only by rows of poplar trees.

The Dutch architect Jan Van Tellingen was called upon to provide his client, a photographer, with a home and work space. A high curved wall, cutting the edifice from north to south, separates the house from the office and photo studio. Following the smaller office in brick and glass, the studio built of black steel is connected to the west end of the facade. The general layout of the three volumes, each one varying in size, stems from the typical Dutch rural design called "Kop-hats-romp" or "Head-neck-torso." Just like the farms in the region, the raised floor plan gives the ensemble the shape of a man lying down.

Inside the main building – the house proper – the function of each room is well defined: openness characterizes the ground floor living areas of sitting room, kitchen and dining room, while upstairs the bedrooms are more closed.

In long vertical bands,
the windows open
horizontally all along the
length of the living room,
letting the fields and
meadows enter into the
interior.

Opposite page
Harmony and rhythm are
the principles behind the
alternation of brick and
glass on the entry
facade.

The architect's choice of materials – glass, white brick and metal – is logical and altogether in line with his Dutch modernist approach. The upstairs is supported by dynamic bright blue pillars on the outside of the glass facade. The openings on this level are reduced to a vertical band and a circular window, set off slightly to the right. The pools surrounding the house and curving around to the east echo the transparency of the facades and the arc of the high wall in the back. Aiming for balance and harmony, the architect has alternated glass expanses with brick walls, straight lines with curves, and juxtaposed black and white.

Through the entrance to the north one enters the large open space of the living/dining room. Where the picture windows meet the wall at an angle, a corner sheltered from the light forms a more intimate nook for dining. In contrast, the dining room table facing the landscape, along with the tiled floor and geometric window frames, create an austere atmosphere of right angles, a mirror image of the patchwork fields that seem to have entered into the room itself. A green plant, taking up the full height of the dining room, underscores this impression of continuity between house and landscape. The red couch adds its touch of warmth amidst these black, white and gray tones. A small white Petra Hartman table and a window display by Alessi betray the signs of the client's penchant for modernity, a modernity more concerned with simplicity, rhythm and regularity, however, than that of rupture and provocation. ◻

In the corner of the
living room the choice
of furniture is daring
considering the
austerity of the space
itself.

Opposite page
The display by Alessi
brings warmth to the
ensemble, as well as
the wooden staircase
leading to the upstairs
bedrooms.

Robert Fink and Peter Martin

A house near Schwyz, Switzerland

An original little temple in front of the main entrance is entirely devoted to the household gods of modern times: the automobile!

Opposite page
To the east, the semicircular balcony above the living room's terrace. This sunny viewpoint is light all day as the sun's rays penetrate through the greenhouse's glass panels. The shape of its roof draws its inspiration from the mountain peaks.

We are in Switzerland's heartland on the peaceful shores of lake Lauerzer, 50 kilometers from Zurich, the Switzerland of wooden chalets and cuckoo clocks; yet there are some surprising discoveries to be made here. Viewed from a helicopter, this symmetrically laid out house in the province of Schwyz resembles a butterfly with outspread wings whose body has been metamorphosed into a long glass casing.

The house sits on a relatively flat site, the result of a man-made embankment, created as a precaution against flooding. Slightly raised and taking up the shores of the lake, it commands superb views of the entire lake and the stunning outline of Mount Mythen in the distance.

Before entering the house proper, one passes through a small Palladian temple, a unique Propylaeum as it were, that has the more prosaic function of housing two garages. Connecting this structure to the main entry is a paved alley protected by a cylindrical glass roof. Beyond this passageway, the eye follows the spiral staircase rising up through the middle of a central greenhouse to the view of the lake. This is the only part of this one-storey house built on two levels. The butterfly-shaped floor plan is perfectly symmetrical, its two wings forming an obtuse angle where we find a covered

The triangular bow-window to the living room.

terrace. Above, a semicircular balcony juts out from the greenhouse, making for an ideal viewpoint.

The central axis makes a separation between the family and the private areas. The kitchen and a large dining/living room, with a marble fireplace separating the two, share one wing. The other, night, wing holds an impressive suite with master bedroom and a luxurious adjoining bathroom, along with the other bedrooms, preceded by their bathroom.

The central greenhouse, like the dwelling's "heart" of glass, irrigates the rest of the house with light. Underpinning this unique central piece is as much a careful analysis of the site as the application of the principles behind the architects' philosophy. Robert Fink and Peter Martin view architecture as governed by two lines of thought: a conceptual framework, including academic canons and contemporary sociological theories, and a formal aspect – the construction's palpable "style" – rooted in history and born of culture but simultaneously stemming from individual experience. If their aim has been to reconcile these two seemingly contradictory elements – as have the most successful examples of the past – they have also incorporated a third element or influence, that of Peter Behrens's theory of "transformed light." Behrens, a German expressionist architect and mentor for, one after the other, Mies Van der Rohe, Gropius and Le Corbusier, was the first to "accustom the eye to recognize the hidden powerful expression of glass and steel."[1]

In addition, local urban planning regulations stipulate that buildings constructed on the lake's shores must not exceed one storey; and considering that in Switzerland one does not take rules lightly, the idea of having a central "heart" of glass seemed at once bright and appealing. And while this structure does have two floors, it could hardly be considered opaque; its function as a source of ventilation and light seemed acceptable enough. Furthermore, as the house opens toward the lake to the east, the terrace on the ground level receives no afternoon light. To compensate for this, the structure is transparent on the upper floor to allow for afternoon light to stream through to the circular balcony which in turn casts the light down through its glass tiled floor to the terrace below, its floor acting as a sort of magnifying glass.

The large amount of glass in this house called for an effective system to ensure the occupants' privacy. There are two forms of blinds for this purpose: blinds with pivoting

---

1. In *Espace, Temps, Architecture* by Siegfried Giedion, Volume 2, Gonthier/Denoël, 1978.

A landscaped garden stretching as far as the lake's shore with the lawn in front of the living room terrace. The incline has been man-made to counter the risk of flooding.

With its perfect balance of colors, the house is like a natural extension of the surrounding mountains.

In line with the living room's bow-window, an almost immaterial structure rises up from the lawn. Probably a support for climbing plants, this structure, apart from its visual appeal, remains a mystery.

Opposite page
Starting from the entry, the general openness of the house becomes apparent. Ahead, the lake and mount Mythen are visible behind the metal staircase. In a symbolic gesture, the curved glass awning above the entranceway takes up the same axis as the greenhouse – the true backbone of the house.

A marble altar in the master bedroom suite replaces
run-of-the-mill bedside tables. Are sacrifices still made
to Venus? Cleverly hidden behind the two oblique
panels are hanging closets.

Opposite page
An impressive marble fireplace separates the living
room from the dining room.

Entirely covered in marble, this luxurious bathroom
seems to have come straight out of a Hollywood set.
Its urban feel is perhaps a little disconcerting
considering the alpine setting. A little more "rusticity"
might well have been welcome here.

vertical slats controlled by cords and blinds regulated by photo-electric light sensitive cells.

The frame of the greenhouse made of steel tubes and the aluminum window frames are painted in turquoise enamel. All the double glazing is transparent except for the upper windows of the winter garden which are tinted to filter the light.

The architects' solutions to this project stem from both esthetic and purely practical considerations. Robert Fink was largely responsible for its technical side, as engineer and foreman, while Peter Martin played a more artistic role. Here, once again, the marriage of heart and reason has borne rich fruit. □

In the dining room the delicate pink of
the marble adds a touch of warmth to
this rather cold universe of white and
green.

Opposite page
The view is even more breathtaking
from the upstairs. One could almost be
on a cruise ship considering the metal
structure of the railing, the curve of the
balcony and the grating on the floor.
The yuccas seem to nod in accord with
this exotic reference.

Biographies

BEHNISCH & PARTNERS

BEHNISCH GÜNTHER

Born in Dresden, Germany, 1922.
Graduated from the Technical
University of Stuttgart in 1951.
Opened his own firm in 1952. From
1966, collaborated with Fritz Auer,
Winfried Büxel, Erhard Tränker,
Karlheinz Weber and, from 1970, with
Manfred Sabatke. In 1979, formed a
partnership with Büxel, Sabatke and
Tränkner under the name Behnisch &
Partners.
Lecturer at the Technische Hochschule
of Darmstadt in 1967, at the
International Academy of Architecture
of Sofia in 1991.
Awarded Gold Medalist by the French
Academy of Architecture in 1992.

Major Works: Munich Olympic
Stadium in collaboration with Frei Otto
(1968-1972). Bonn: federal parlement
building (1983-1992). Frankfurt: German
Post Office museum (1984). Stuttgart:
Hysolar Institute (1985-1987). Since
1954 in Germany, some fifty projects
for schools, high schools and
professional training centers, including,
most recently, the St-Benno
Gymnasium in Dresden, a Montessori
school and the Münster nursery school
in Ingolstadt-Hollerstauden (1996).
Private homes: Behnisch in Kemnat,
Gackstatter in Stuttgart-Weilimdorf
(1969) and Charlotte in Stuttgart-
Sillenbuch (1993).

CARDENAL JOAN CARLES

Born in Barcelona, 1929.
Graduated from the ETSAB in 1964.
Opened his own firm in 1983.
Coordinating architect for the Olympic
Games sports arena in Barcelona
alongside head architect, Arata Isozaki
(1986-1992).

Major Works: Science faculty for the
University of Barcelona (1984), the
restoration of the Gornal industrial
building in Hospitalet del Llobregat
(1991).

DI FRANCO ELIO

Born in Bisceglie, Italy, 1954.
Graduated from the Architecture
Faculty of Florence.
Opened his own firm in Florence in
1984.
Designer of exhibitions, Di Franco also
creates design objects for Zanotta,
Sisal Collezioni, Galotti & Redice,
R.S.V.P.

Major Works: Casa Santilini in Blera
(1993) and Loggia Chiara in Arezzo
(1996).

DÖRING WOLFGANG

Born in Berlin, 1934.
Studied at the Technische Hochschule
in Munich, then in Darmstadt.
Opened his own firm in Dusseldorf in
1964.
Published *Perspektiven einer
Architektur* in 1970.
Professor at the Technische
Hochschule d'Aix-la-Chapelle since
1973.

Major Works: Wabbel residence (1965)
and Dom Business Hotel (1980-1984) in
Düsseldorf; Döring appartment (1983-
1984) in Bonn.

FINK, MARTIN & ASSOCIATES

FINK ROBERT

Born in Biel, Switzerland, 1947.
Graduated from Zurich University in
1972.
Opened his own firm in Schwyz in
1976. Reorganized in 1992 in
partnership with Peter Martin.

MARTIN PETER

Born in London, 1951.
Graduated from Oxford University in
design in 1975.
Became Robert Fink's main partner in
1992.

GALI BETH

Born in Barcelona, 1950.
Graduated from the Escola Tecnica
Superior d'Arquitectura of Barcelona in
1982.
Vice President of the ADI-FAD from
1976-1979.
City architect for Barcelona from 1982-
1988. Directed the Olympic Games'
sites: Montjuic, Diagonal and Vall
d'Hebron from 1988-1992.
Professor at ETSAB in the urban design
department since 1994.
ADI-FAD Gold Delta Award in 1966 and
1969 for her design objects. Recipient
of numerous FAD awards, including
FAD 1995 in the ephemeral
architecture section.

Major Works: Joan Miró park and
library (1982-1990), city information
office (1984), Emili Vendrell gardens,
Casa Cases apartments (1982-1989),
Fossar de la Pedrera park, Migdia park
and its open-air auditorium (1992),
restoration of the Maria Cristina
avenue, Indumentaria fashion boutique,
all in Barcelona; Zafra park in Huelva;
development of the Hertogenbosh and
Roermond historical centers in Holland.

JOURDA & PERRAUDIN

JOURDA FRANÇOISE-HÉLÈNE

Born in 1955.
Graduated in architecture in 1979.
Lectured at the School of Architecture
in Lyon (1979-1983), Saint-Étienne
(1985-1989), Oslo (1990), at the
University of Minesota (1992) and since
1997, at the University of Kassel in
Germany.

PERRAUDIN GILLES

Born in 1949.
Graduated in architecture in 1977.
Lectured at the School of Architecture
in Lyon (1977-1981) and in Oslo (1990).
Professor at the School of Architecture
of Montpellier.

Major Works: Lanterne school

complex in Cergy-Pontoise (1985); Lyon
School of Architecture (1987) in Vaulx-
en-Velin; Parilly metro station (1988) in
Vénissieux; experimental houses in
Stuttgart; housing in Tassin-la-Demi-
Lune; offices and housing at the ZAC
Didot in Paris; Cité Scolaire
Internationale (1989) and urban
equipment for the city of Lyon (1990);
University of Marne-la-Vallée (1992);
hall of Justice of Melun (1994). Park
and greenhouse for BUGA in Potsdam
(1997).

KOVATSCH MANFRED

Born in Villach, Austria, 1940.
Established practice in Munich.
Studied at the Technische Hochschule
in Graz. Graduated from Berkeley.
Professor at the Fine Art Academy of
Munich since 1986.

LACKNER JOSEF

Born in Tyrol, 1931.
Graduated in architecture in 1952.
Realized most of his projects in the
Tyrol, Baviera, Westphalia, Bade-
Wurtemberg and in Vienna.

LORENZ PETER

Born in Innsbruck, Austria, 1950.
Doctor in architecture, Venice, 1984.
Opened his Innsbruck office in 1980
and a second in Vienna in 1991.
Lectured at the University of Innsbruck
(1988-1990), in Salzburg (1991) and in
India in 1994 at the Universities of New
Delhi, Bombay and Ahmedabad.

Major Works: in Innsbruck, multi-
storey housing complex in Peergründe
(1983-1984), the Menardi House (1985-
1988), the renovation and extension of
the Alt-Innsbrugg Town Hall (1988-
1995), the Kohlstatturm (1987-1995);
Das Triest hotel, Vienna (1991-1994).

MECANOO ARCHITEKTEN

Firm created in 1984 in Delft, Holland,
by five young graduates of the School
of Architecture of the University of
Technology: Henk Döll, Erick Van
Egeraat, Francine Houbel, Roelf
Steenhuis and Chris de Weijer.

Major Works: in Rotterdam, housing
and commercial complex in Kruisplein
(1985), Hillekop and Tiendplein (1989),
restaurant "de Boompjes" (1990),
Ringvaartplasbuurt Oost housing
(1993); botanical laboratory and library
for the University of Agriculture (1992)
in Wageningen; Herdenkingsplein
housing in Maastricht (1994); public
library in Almelo (1994); Isala college in
Silvolde (1995), Business and
management faculty in Utrecht (1995).

MENDINI ALESSANDRO

Designer, born in Milan, 1931.
Mendini has designed a number of
objects and pieces of furniture for
Alessi, Philips, Swatch, etc.
In 1989, created Studio Mendini with
his brother Francesco in Milan.
Directed the design magazines,

Casabella, Modo and Domus.

Major Works: the Alessi House (House of Happiness), tower building in Hiroshima, Groninguen Museum in Holland, the theater in Arezzo, Italy.

MORO PAOLO & FRANCESCO

MORO PAOLO

Born in Geneva, 1945.
Graduated from the Technical School in Lugano in 1966.
Since 1967, has worked with Luigi Snozzi and Livio Vacchini in Locarno and with Arthur Bugna in Geneva.
Opened his own firm in 1974. Joined his brother Francesco in partnership, 1976.

MORO FRANCESCO

Born in Sorengo,1948.
Graduated from the School of Architecture at the Univesity of Geneva.
From 1977, lectured at the Univesity of Geneva.
Worked in partnership with the Moreno-Escolari studio in Geneva.
Joined his brother Paolo in partnership, 1976.

RODON JOAN

Born in Barcelona, 1956.
Graduated from ETSAB in 1981.
Opened his own firm in 1982.
Winner of the 1994 FAD award from the critics and the public for his reading rooms at the Catalonia Library in Barcelona.

Major Works: Catalonia Library, Romea Theater, Civic Center in Poligono Gornal, Polytechnic Institute in Vilanova i la Geltru, all in Barcelona. Arauz House in Vallvidrera, Juvany House in Areu and the Cala Aiguafreda in Begur.

SCHNEIDER-WESSLING ERICH

Born in Wessling, Germany, 1931.
Graduated from the Technische Hochschule, Munich in 1956 and from the University of Southern California.
Worked for Richard J. Neutra in Los Angeles and in Maracaibo, Venezuela (1956-1958); for Frank Lloyd Wright in Taliesin West in Arizona (1957).
Opened his own firm in Cologne in 1961.
From 1972, lectured at the Munich Fine Art Academy which he presided from 1979 to 1982.

SNOZZI LUIGI

Born in Mendrisio, Switzerland, 1932.
Graduated from the Technische Hochschule, Zurich in 1957.
Opened his own firm in 1958 in Locarno.
In 1962-1971, worked in partnership with Lino Vacchini.
In 1975, founded a firm with Bruno Jenni in Zurich.
In 1988, founded a new firm in Lausanne.

Major Works: low income housing (1965-1966), the Bianchetti House (1975-1977), in Locarno; Cavalli House in Verscio (1976-1978); the Kalmann House in Brione (1976-1977), Bianchini House in Brissago (1984-1986), the Bernasconi House in Corona (1988-1989); Reiffersen Bank, gymnasium and the Guidotti House in Monte Carasso.

SPRENG & PARTNER ARCHITEKTEN

SPRENG DANIEL

Swiss architect established in Bern.

Major Works: in Bern, boutiques for Jutta van D., Dr. Horber house, "House with studio" and conference room, offices and cafeteria for the Federal Building department; Bally International Design Center in Schönewerd; hotel in Martel, France.

VAN TELLINGEN JAN

Born in Zeist, Holland.
Graduated from the Academy of Architectural Design, Utrecht.
Opened an interior design firm in 1974.
In 1980, joined the firm of Mazairac/Boonzaaijer & Partners, reorganized into Mazairac/Boonzaaijer & Van Tellingen.

Major Works: numerous bungalows; interior decoration for the Trade Center in Nieuweigen, for the House of the Future in Rosmalen, and for the Office of the Future in Den Bosch.

WAGNER MARTIN

Born in Basel, 1947.
Graduated from the Technical School in Brugg-Windisch.
Worked in the firm of Dolf Schnebli in Agno. Partner with Max Wagner in Basel, then with Martin Schmidt in Carona and Fredi Meier in Zurich, before opening his own firm in Basel.

Bibliography

General Reference
AMSONEIT Wolfgang, *Contemporary European Architects*, Benedikt Taschen, Cologne, 1994.
BLASER Werner , *Architecture 70/80 in Switzerland*, Birkhäuser Verlag, Basel, 1982.
BOGA Thomas, *Tessiner Architekten – Bauten und Entwürfe 1960-1985*, ETH Zurich, 1986.
CARIOU Joël, *Maisons d'architectes*, volumes I and II, Alternatives, Paris, 1994 and 1996.
KUZ Zehra, Chramosta Walter M. and Frampton Kenneth, *Autochtone Architektur in Tyrol*, Ernst Bliem, Hall-in-Tyrol, 1992.
ZABALBEASCOA Anatxu, *The New Spanish Architecture,* Rizzoli, New York, 1992.
L'Architecture espagnole contemporaine. Les Années 80, Gustavo Gili éd., Barcelona, 1991.

Monographs
Gauzin-Müller Dominique,*Behnish & Partners. 50 Years of Architecture*, Academy Editions, 1997.
Elio di Franco, exhibition catalogue, Libria/Melfi, Matera, 1997.
"Gali Beth" in *Architectural Houses, City Houses,* volume II, Atrium, Barcelona, 1991.
Jourda & Perraudin, Mardaga/Institut Français d'Architecture, Paris, 1993.
Joan Rodon Arquitecto, Axis, Barcelona, 1995.
Snozzi Vacchini Galfetti, *Three Architects from Ticino*, exhibition catalogue, Finnish Architecture Museum, Helsinki, 1990.

Photo credits

Pages 124 to 131: photos Gabriele Basilico
Pages 8 to 15: photos Günther Behnisch
Pages 16 to 23: photos Christine Blaser/Susana Bruell
Pages 106 to 113, 114 to 123, 132 à 141: photos Reiner Blunck
Pages 24 to 31: photos Mario Ciampi
Pages 38 to 45: photos Stéphane Couturier/Archipress
Pages 52 to 59: photos Ferran Freixa
Pages 76 to 81, 98 to105: photos Giancarlo Gardin
Pages 32 to 37 and back cover: photos Elmar Joeressen
Pages 148 to 157: photos Peter Martin and Fritz Matti
Pages 82 to 89: photos Occhiomagico
Pages 90 to 97: photos John Parker
Pages 60 to 67 and front cover: photos Eugèni Pons
Pages 142 to 147: photos Hennie Raaymakers
Pages 46 to 51: photos Scagliola, Brakkee, Francine Houben
Pages 6, 68 to 75: photos Francesc Tur

Printed in Italy